MW00342300

# Getting It Done: A Guide for Government Executives

## 2017 Edition

# Getting It Done: A Guide for Government Executives

## 2017 Edition

MARK A. ABRAMSON

DANIEL J. CHENOK

JOHN M. KAMENSKY

ROWMAN & LITTLEFIELD PUBLISHERS, INC.

*Lanham • Boulder • New York • London*

ROWMAN & LITTLEFIELD PUBLISHERS, INC.

Published in the United States of America
by Rowman & Littlefield Publishers, Inc.
A wholly owned subsidiary of The Rowman & Littlefield Publishing Group, Inc.
4501 Forbes Boulevard, Suite 200, Lanham, Maryland 20706
www.rowmanlittlefield.com

Unit A, Whitacre Mews, 26-34 Stannary Street, London SE11 4AB

Copyright © 2009, 2013, 2016 by Rowman & Littlefield Publishers, Inc.

*All rights reserved*. No part of this publication may be reproduced,
stored in a retrieval system, or transmitted in any form or by any
means, electronic, mechanical, photocopying, recording, or otherwise,
without the prior permission of the publisher.

British Library Cataloguing in Publication Information Available

**Library of Congress Cataloging-in-Publication Data Available**

ISBN-13: 978-1-4422-7360-3 (cloth : alk. paper)
ISBN-10: 1-4422-7360-7 (cloth : alk. paper)
ISBN-13: 978-1-4422-7361-0 (pbk. : alk. paper)
ISBN-10: 1-4422-7361-5 (pbk. : alk. paper)
ISBN-13: 978-1-4422-7362-7 (electronic)
ISBN-10: 1-4422-7362-3 (electronic)

Printed in the United States of America

♾™ The paper used in this publication meets the minimum requirements of American
National Standard for Information Sciences—Permanence of Paper for Printed Library
Materials, ANSI/NISO Z39.48-1992.

# TABLE OF CONTENTS

# FOREWORD

In 2009, the IBM Center for The Business of Government released *Getting It Done: A Guide for Government Executives* as a guide for new leaders, especially new political appointees. This book helped new government executives acclimate quickly to the world of public service as practiced in Washington, D.C., and it contained a series of short strategic discussions about "dos and don'ts," along with insights about working with key stakeholders from experienced political executives. *Getting It Done* was revised and reissued as a second edition in 2013. Over the last eight years, *Getting It Done* has been widely read, ordered, and reordered as a must-read roadmap for government leaders to hit the ground running.

With the advent of a new administration in 2017, a new set of leaders will arrive across the federal government. The government that they will lead has changed in many ways from the government inherited by the Obama Administration in 2009. Accordingly, this 2017 edition of *Getting It Done* has been updated to reflect the changes. Part I introduces current perspectives on what to do (and what to avoid) to succeed; Part II contains a series of new essays on key stakeholders by experienced government professionals who have "been there" and "gotten it done."

We would like to thank two individuals who were instrumental in the previous editions of *Getting It Done*: G. Martin Wagner and Jonathan D. Breul. While serving as a Senior Fellow at the IBM Center, Marty Wagner drafted the initial Part I insights on "to dos" based on his 30-year government career. Many of his insights continue to be timeless. Jonathan Breul, former Executive Director of the IBM Center, was a key participant in both previous editions, and among many contributions was responsible for developing the stakeholder map contained in the book.

New government leaders have a great opportunity to make a positive difference for the nation. We hope that the 2017 edition to *Getting It Done* will prove useful in helping them to achieve success.


Daniel J. Chenok
Executive Director
IBM Center for The Business of Government

# INTRODUCTION

This book has been written for those who have answered the call to public service. We deeply appreciate your willingness to work on the nation's greatest problems.

Those new to government will find a world very different than their previous experience in other sectors. Those returning to government will find a far different government than the one they left. Both will find a large group of stakeholders, including members of the United States Congress, very interested in every action they take. In addition, you will face the challenge of managing large organizations. If cabinet departments were listed in the Fortune 500, they would occupy slots in the top 20.

The goal of this book is to assist political executives, as well as career executives new to their position, in navigating the current political environment and the world of Washington. The waters are likely to be turbulent. If one does successfully succeed in managing in Washington, it will be a very rewarding and fulfilling experience.

Part I contains seven "to-dos" necessary to "get it done" in Washington. Part II consists of 14 chapters, each describing an important stakeholder in the political environment of Washington.


## Seven "To-Dos"

Part I presents a straightforward to-do list to guide you in your new leadership position:

- **Before confirmation, be careful.** There is likely to be a gap in time (sometimes long) between nomination and confirmation. During this time period, learn as much about your agency as possible. In addition, be careful throughout this time period to avoid making commitments or decisions prior to being officially confirmed.
- **Learn how things work.** While you have done your background research on your agency prior to your confirmation, devote your early days in office to learning more about your customers, your agency programs, and "flash points" that may cause problems down the road for your agency.
- **Act quickly.** As part of learning how your agency works, find out what needs quick action by you and what issues require further study. You will learn much from talking with your staff and stakeholders about how your agency is performing and what actions you need to take quickly.
- **Develop a vision and a focused agenda.** A vision and a focused agenda will be crucial to your success in Washington. You will need to both communicate the vision and convey a sense of urgency to get it done.

- **Assemble your leadership team.** A key ingredient to your success will be putting together a *joint* political/career team. Don't view your staff as two distinct camps (political and career). Avoid "political appointees only" meetings as much as possible. Your job is to get these two groups working together as one management team committed to your vision and your agency's goals.
- **Deliver results.** Once you have created a vision, focused agenda, and a good leadership team, there will be many distractions. Delivering on promises not only will take discipline, but also a set of decision-making and operational processes. Leverage existing processes and networks where possible. Ensure that day-to-day operations are effective, but don't try to manage them yourself or you'll quickly lose perspective and your focus on your vision and results. Also, keeping a focus on measurable results makes it easier to make your case with key stakeholders.
- **Manage your environment.** All organizations—public and private—have stakeholders and a complex environment, but many observers think that government is harder because there are so many stakeholders. Part II discusses 14 major stakeholders with whom you will be dealing. The key to your success will be succeeding (to a large extent) with all of them. Failure to work effectively with any one group can likely lessen your chances of success in government and possibly shorten your tenure.

## Seven "To-Dos" for Getting It Done

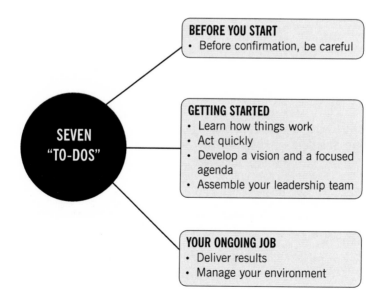

**SEVEN "TO-DOS"**

**BEFORE YOU START**
- Before confirmation, be careful

**GETTING STARTED**
- Learn how things work
- Act quickly
- Develop a vision and a focused agenda
- Assemble your leadership team

**YOUR ONGOING JOB**
- Deliver results
- Manage your environment

## Fourteen Stakeholders for Getting It Done

**YOUR BOSSES**
- White House
- White House Policy Councils
- Office of Management and Budget
- Congress

**YOUR COLLEAGUES**
- Cross-Agency Collaborators
- Interagency Councils
- Office of Personnel Management

**YOUR GOALS**

**YOUR CONSTITUENCIES**
- Citizens
- Unions
- State, Local, and Tribal Governments
- Interest Groups and Associations

**YOUR OVERSEERS**
- Government Accountability Office
- Inspectors General
- Media

## Stakeholders

Part II of this book provides overviews of the 14 stakeholder groups you will most frequently encounter while in government. We grouped these stakeholders into four clusters: your bosses, your colleagues, your constituencies, and your overseers. While some groups might appear in two categories (Congress is your boss *and* oversees your organization), this framework is useful to understanding your relationship with each one.

### Your bosses

It is often said that one of the major differences between the public and private sectors is that you have many bosses in government. While the assertion that you have 535 bosses in Congress might be slightly overstated, there is much truth to it. In Washington, any one of the 535 members of Congress (or any of their 30,000 staff) can make your life easier by supporting your agency—or more difficult by providing your agency with a directive or a new piece of legislation placing restrictions or limitations on what your agency can do.

Closer to home, however, are three distinct parts of the White House on which your job literally depends. First, there is the White House itself. While you will see the president infrequently, you will often encounter a variety of special assistants to the president, each of whom works in a different White House office. They can be enormously helpful and supportive to you once you develop a good working relationship with them.

Second, we focus on the three White House Policy Councils (the National Security Council, the Domestic Policy Council, and the National Economic Council). These councils have become increasingly important in recent years as the White House has assumed a greater leadership and coordinative role in new policy initiatives.

Last, but by no means least, is the Office of Management and Budget (OMB), which coordinates the development of administration policies and decides on how much funding your agency can request from Congress. In addition, OMB will be involved in many other aspects of your position, such as reviewing proposed legislation or your testimony before Congress, as well as overseeing regulations you might propose. As in all organizations, working with your bosses is essential to your success in government.

## Your colleagues

While you will constantly be working upward with your bosses, you might not be as aware of the importance of working sideways with your colleagues. In government, you cannot overestimate the importance of your colleagues. There are likely to be few instances in which you and your agency can make a decision solely by yourselves (even after consultation with your bosses). More common is the scenario in which your bosses will actively seek the opinion and concurrence of your colleagues in other agencies across government.

In the chapter on cross-agency collaborators, we recommend that you set the right tone in creating the expectation that your management team will work closely with other departments and agencies. The chapter on inter-agency councils recommends that you participate actively on interagency councils that invite you to become a member. You must, however, assume a different role in your participation on interagency councils. Instead of being the boss of your organization, you become a peer and colleague working on government-wide issues.

While it has an oversight function, we have placed the Office of Personnel Management (OPM) in the colleague grouping. We recommend that you reach out to OPM to help you and your agency seek human capital flexibilities that can assist you in better accomplishing your agency's mission. While OPM provides specific services to your agency, you can also work with them as colleagues to achieve your mission.

## Your constituencies

Each agency will have its own unique set of constituencies. In Part I (Seven "To-Dos") we note that different constituency groups cluster around your agency. We have not attempted to map the specific groups that will have an interest in your particular agency. Your staff will be able to describe these groups to you, and you will soon be meeting with them to get acquainted and to begin building effective partnership relationships.

Instead, we have focused on a cross-cutting set of constituencies. There are the citizens, with whom you will interact in two ways. First, some citizens will be your customers, and we recommend in Part I that you meet with customers to assess their satisfaction with your agency and whether the delivery of services to them can be improved. Second, citizens are in fact the ultimate bosses of government and indeed have major stakes in the government policies and programs. In our Part II chapter on citizens, we recommend that you use social media and other new tools to engage citizens on new policies or programs you are considering.

Turning to the internal side of your organization, we discuss the importance of unions as a constituency. If your agency is represented by one or more unions, develop a collaborative working relationship with them.

While government executives are becoming increasingly attuned to the importance of collaborating with other federal agencies, the next major challenge is for the federal government to develop more effective working relationships with state, local, and tribal governments. Federal spending will become much tighter in future years. As a consequence, government leaders will need to find new ways to accomplish national objectives through partnerships with states, localities, and nonprofit organizations.

Finally, there are the traditional interest groups and associations. As noted above, you will quickly get to know the organizations interested in your agency. In the chapter on interest groups and associations, we stress the importance of these groups as a valuable information resource for you. There will clearly be differences of opinions between you and these groups. The key to a successful relationship will not be agreement on all issues, but instead your ability to create an ongoing dialogue with them and to maintain a constant exchange of information between you and the organizations.

## Your overseers

In addition to looking upward to your bosses and sideways at your colleagues and constituencies, you will also need to look over your shoulder at your overseers. Oversight organizations are a fact of life in government. Ongoing scrutiny of how public funds are spent will become a daily part of your life. While it is all too easy to fall into an adversarial relationship with your overseers, you should work hard to develop an effective working relationship with them.

The most well-known oversight, or watchdog, organization is the Government Accountability Office (GAO), previously known as the General Accounting Office. In the chapter on GAO, we place the emphasis on your using GAO as a valuable information resource. While your staff, including your GAO liaison, will be busy working with GAO on specific GAO reviews underway in your agency, you can use information contained in prior and ongoing GAO studies to identify problem areas that Congress is likely to ask you about and areas that your agency will need to work on.

The second watchdog organization you will encounter is the independent Office of the Inspector General in your department or agency. Past relationships between IGs and agency heads have ranged from outright hostility to a cooperative partnership. Like GAO, IGs can identify problem areas that your agency needs to focus on.

Third, you will encounter the media. The Washington media are unique. You will have an able press staff to assist you in both your proactive and reactive relationships with the media. Like all the stakeholders discussed in Part II, the media can assist you greatly in getting your message out and communicating your vision to those both inside and outside of government. As with all the stakeholders discussed, time spent with the media will be a good investment.

## A Final Word

Simply put, Washington is a tough town. Succeeding in Washington requires not only hard work (which is clearly needed), but also highly sensitive antennae about the environment surrounding your agency. We have not attempted to rank-order the stakeholders discussed in this book. Instead, we have provided groupings as a way for you to organize your approach to each of the stakeholders.

Unlike baseball, where you don't have to get a hit every time at bat to be a success, government actually does require you to bat 1.000. You must succeed with all 14 of the stakeholder groups described in this book. Any one of them can cause problems for you. Conversely, every one of them can serve as a key leverage point for you to succeed in Washington. The goal of this volume is assisting you in effectively using these levers.

# PART I: SEVEN "TO-DOs"

*Part I draws primarily on the insights of G. Martin Wagner, who drafted the original 2009 version of this section.*

**CHAPTER ONE**

# Before Confirmation, Be Careful

# BEFORE CONFIRMATION, BE CAREFUL

Congratulations on your appointment in the new administration. You are taking on more than a job; as you know, it is an opportunity to have an important impact on our society and the world. You are here to deliver on the new administration's programs, but you are answering to a higher calling as well. The oath you swear upon your appointment is not to the president you serve. The oath is to "support and defend the Constitution of the United States." You are part of the administration, but you are part of something greater as well.

Unfortunately, the period of time between your nomination and confirmation (when you can actually start your job) will likely be a long one—perhaps several months or longer. It is not uncommon for delays due to factors that have nothing to do with either you or your agency. Frequently, a group of nominations may get "bundled" together and require negotiations between the White House and Congress to resolve specific issues that may or may not be related to your agency.

While waiting for confirmation, you may be tempted to start getting engaged in the work of your agency. This is almost always a bad idea as it tends to incur congressional displeasure and can compromise your being confirmed at all. It is better to use this time to get to know your future agency and the issues it faces. Many agency decisions can be deferred until you are confirmed.

While waiting to get started officially, learning more about your future agency and its environment will be time well spent. Being effective in Washington begins with understanding how Washington works. Everyone understands the importance of politics, but it is also important to understand how the political and programmatic interact. The roles of stakeholders, the bureaucracy, and process are critical. Washington tends to have large numbers of stakeholders influencing outcomes around your programs in ways that may be difficult to discern. Effective strategies are built on understanding and leveraging the many competing interests you will find, including those that are not supportive. A good beginning is critical.

### Use your time before confirmation to collect information, but avoid decision making.

As noted above, use your time prior to confirmation to get as much information as you can about your agency and department, your key stakeholders, the key issues, and how things work. You can meet with people in your new organization, but it is preferable to do so in a different building than the one in which your agency is located.

Prior to confirmation, don't be offended if your agency briefers sometimes hold back information that will be available to you once you are confirmed. They are restricted by law as to what they can share with you until you are confirmed. You cannot make decisions until you have the authority to do so. Prudence is warranted in this time period.

## Learn who in Congress affects your agency, how they affect it, and their points of view.

It is likely that multiple committees will oversee your agency. Authorization, appropriations, and perhaps multiple oversight committees in both the Senate and the House will be important to you. Your legislative staff will be able to brief you on which committees have jurisdiction over what issues, the views of the majority and the minority sides of each committee, the views of specific members, the topics that are driven by staff concerns, and the issues that are especially important to specific members. Understanding Congress is a full-time job, so you will probably want to make sure you have a good legislative team.

## Start to build good relations with the Hill, but don't make commitments too soon.

A good relationship with Congress will help you get confirmed and will be critical to your success once you are in your agency. You will be making courtesy calls on Congress after you are nominated. Use these meetings to get to know the principals from both parties and their staffs as well. A senator's or representative's staff can be as important as the elected official on many issues. A good relationship will later be important to resolving the inevitable conflicts that will arise between the executive and legislative branches.

You may find that members of Congress want you to make commitments for the agency. Be attentive to their requests, but don't make commitments too soon. A "too soon" commitment may often have unforeseen consequences, and it is a good idea to consult with your staff-to-be to understand what those consequences may be. Tell members of Congress you will look into the question and get back to them. Do, however, make sure to get back to them after your confirmation.

## Limit your endorsement of previous agency positions on issues until you have had time to assess them.

Your staff-to-be will be helping to prepare you for your confirmation hearings. Some may encourage you to embrace the agency's prior policies. Avoid doing this to the extent you can until you have had a chance to understand the issues.

Confirmation hearings are about your qualifications for the job. They are not about justifying what the agency has done in the past—notwithstanding the briefing books the agency is giving you which do just that. A good way to frame an answer to a confirmation question on a prior agency position would be: "I have not had an opportunity yet to study the specifics of this issue in depth, but in similar situations I have done the following ..."

**Start to get to know your agency, but avoid the briefing book trap.**

Your staff-to-be will be preparing briefing materials for you. Usually, these are loose leaf notebooks that explain the agency and its priorities in exhaustive detail. The details in the book make for excellent reference materials, but sometimes they are poor guides into the most important or most urgent issues.

Follow a focused approach in this time period. Your first priority is to get confirmed with as few constraining commitments as possible. Your second priority is to get a head start on understanding the important issues facing your agency. Concentrate on understanding those issues of concern to the Hill, and use that as a path to understanding the agency as a whole.

Request that your staff structures the briefing process to fit how you like to learn. Some people like to read papers, others like to have a conversation, still others learn best from a briefing. Tell your agency staff what style works best for you and they will be glad to adjust to your preference.

You should use the detailed agency briefing books as key reference materials. But remember that briefing books are only one source of information for you. The briefing books will give your agency's point of view. Though important, it should be augmented with the views of customers and stakeholders. You may also want to learn what your departmental inspector general (IG) and the Government Accountability Office (GAO) have said about your agency. GAO may be briefing the Hill, and what they say may come up in your confirmation hearings. So time spent reviewing prior GAO reports on your agency will be time well spent.

**Read your agency's enabling legislation.**

Finally, ask staff to pull together a copy of your agency's enabling legislation. It may not be easy reading, but it does lay out what authorities Congress has granted (or withheld). You may also ask about reauthorization legislation that may be pending or coming up in the next two years. Having a baseline understanding will be helpful as you read your briefing books!

---

# Takeaways

- Use your time before confirmation to collect information, but avoid decision making.
- Learn who in Congress affects your agency, how they affect it, and their points of view.
- Start to build good relations with the Hill, but don't make commitments too soon.
- Limit your endorsement of previous agency positions on issues until you have had time to assess them.
- Start to get to know your agency, but avoid the briefing book trap.
- Read your agency's enabling legislation.

## CHAPTER TWO

# Learn How Things Work

# LEARN HOW THINGS WORK

Your agency is a large bureaucracy with a large number of career employees and relatively few political appointees. Most of the programs are managed by career executives who typically have been with the agency longer than you will be there. The bureaucracy is both the means by which you will achieve program success and a separate culture that will support your agenda and give continuity between administrations.

You will learn that process is king, so learn about the process. How you make a decision can be as important as the decision itself. There are processes to buy, to hire, to regulate, and to solicit advice. There are even processes to speed up the process. Successfully implementing your agency programs will depend, in part, on mastering these processes rather than letting the processes master you.

Being successful will require the ability to maneuver among and leverage the various competing interests, while overseeing a complex bureaucracy and using existing processes that can stand scrutiny. You must focus on the important few priorities while keeping the less important ones from occupying all your time or, worse, blowing up into a full-fledged crisis that thwarts your agenda and tarnishes your legacy.

To get things done, you will need to understand your customers. You will also need to understand your stakeholders, what they want and don't want, and how they influence outcomes. You will need to understand the tools your agency has available and their limitations. You will need to understand enough about how your agency operates to be able to use those tools effectively.

### Learn what your agency's customers want.

Your agency has customers. You should find out who your agency's customers are and what they want. Talk to representatives of the different customer communities to get a handle on their concerns and understand how they view your agency. In many cases, other federal agencies and state and local governments have programs that overlap with your own and affect the same customers. As a result, agencies are finding it more important to work together. Understanding these overlaps is important. In addition, ask your staff about what they think customers want and compare it with what you are hearing directly.

### Develop an understanding of your agency's programs and how they achieve the outcomes you want.

You will need an understanding of how your agency delivers programs to customers. This will also require an understanding of the role of the stakeholders in those programs because program delivery involves both your customers and your stakeholders. You will also need a high-level understanding of how your agency operates to deliver these programs. Your agency follows complex internal procedures as part of its normal way of operating. In many cases, these are dictated by laws and regulations, but sometimes they are simply the standard procedures that have been followed in the past. You don't want to get lost in that complexity, but you need to know the dimensions of program delivery.

Your career staff understands that complexity and knows how to get things done within the bureaucracy. Get them to help you understand the internal operations of your agency and how you can get it to do what you want. The civil servants you choose to work with closely should have an understanding of the internal processes of your agency, an understanding of what you want to do, and an ability to help focus your leadership on those who most need to be led. The right ones can also help modernize those processes to better keep with the needs of today's government.

## Understand your agency's career workforce.

Before taking your new position, you should undertake research on your agency's workforce:

- Find out your agency workforce's trends in its demographics, skill mix, pending retirements, succession planning for career executives, and any critical skill gaps.
- Find out your employees' "level of engagement" from recent surveys.

The federal government annually surveys the entire federal workforce regarding a range of issues, via the Office of Personnel Management. The survey of employee attitudes and perceptions provides data going back a decade, so you can see changes in trends and comparisons between agencies.

Don't just look at the top-level numbers but also at the range of responses on key questions between different components within your agency, such as ratings of trust in top leadership and frontline supervisors, and employees' degree of engagement in their work and mission.

The nonprofit Partnership for Public Service annually analyzes the OPM data, grouping agencies with similar missions together for comparisons and ranking agency components from best to worst place to work, etc. Ask your staff for relevant summaries.

Why is this important? A recent study of past reports by the Government Accountability Office shows that the root cause for why many agencies tend to be at a high risk for fraud, waste, and mismanagement can be traced back to an inadequate or under-skilled workforce.

## Understand that your workforce also may have a large contract workforce.

You should recognize that your workforce is not just civil servants, but it also includes a mix of contractors. You should find out who your major contractors are, where their staffs are located (sometimes they are mixed in with your staff, perhaps even outside your office), and to what extent they may be a critical player in selected areas of your agency's mission delivery. Agencies will vary from just a few contractors to upwards of 90 percent of their workforce.

## Learn what stakeholders want and how they affect your programs.

What your customers want is only part of the story. What stakeholders want can be equally important, and much of this book is devoted to discussing the perspectives of stakeholders with whom you will be working throughout your time in office. By stakeholders, we mean any person or organization that is not your agency's customer but has an interest in what your agency does.

The top-level stakeholder is Congress, through its constitutionally established relationship with the executive branch; but it is also a conduit for other stakeholder concerns. Your agency will need to work with the White House, the Office of Management and Budget (OMB), and other agencies and the various interagency policy councils.

A set of stakeholders that have an interest in how you support them will surround your customers. These can be the companies that support your customers, public interest groups, or state and local governments.

Your agency will also face reviews from the Government Accountability Office and your agency's Office of Inspector General. Finally, the media are stakeholders, but in a unique way. They make issues more visible, are conduits for other stakeholder concerns, and tend to frame issues in whatever way makes a more compelling story.

Your most important relationships will be agency-specific. For example, there is no single stakeholder called industry. In reading Part II (Stakeholders), keep in mind that the most important stakeholder relationships will be those specific to your agency. Delivering any important program requires addressing stakeholder interests as well as meeting citizen or customer needs. Understanding who the stakeholders are, what their interests are, and how they affect outcomes will be critical to developing a strategy to get things done.

It is difficult to overstate the importance of stakeholders to your success. Many programs have foundered when an interested party persuaded Congress to block some action, oftentimes occurring with no clear picture of who did it or how it was done. Your colleagues in the White House can weigh in on your programs, but they may not agree with each other. The Office of Management and Budget has an enormous impact on your resources and is also intertwined with the internal operations of your agency.

Finally, keep in mind that many stakeholders have a vested interest in the status quo you are planning to change. Talk to the stakeholders; find out their concerns. Get briefed by your staff on those concerns and on how stakeholders intervene in your programs. Talk to your predecessors and find out from all of them how stakeholders weigh in. Each perspective will be a bit different, but combining those perspectives will give you a more complete picture.

### Learn how the media affect your programs.

Part of program delivery is conveying the value of the program and responding to its critics. Perception is important, and often the coverage of an event or program in the media creates a perception of events. Take the press seriously. Try to understand how they have framed your agency's issues in the past so you can work to frame them the way you want to in the future. This is an area where talking to your predecessors can be particularly useful.

We offer the following four insights:

- The media will give more play to an agency mistake than an agency accomplishment. Efforts to change that are likely to be futile.
- Most stories in the mainstream press involve a hero and a villain, so finding a way to make your agency the hero can be a good strategy.

---

## Political Appointees' Impressions of Careerists

| First Impressions | Later Impressions |
|---|---|
| *"[At first,] they were skeptical of me and our agenda."* | *"They wanted to play in the policy process."* |
| *"Very risk averse."* | *"The civil servants really trained me."* |
| *"Seemed tentative and afraid to give their real opinions."* | *"They really responded to good management."* |
| *"Too much focus on process."* | *"Most of them understood that I belonged at the table to fight for certain policies."* |
| *"They seemed very eager to please."* | |
| *"Some of the careerists thought we were crazy!"* | |

From "Getting to Know You: Rules of Engagement for Political Appointees and Career Executives" by Joseph A. Ferrara and Lynn C. Ross. In *Learning the Ropes: Insights for Political Appointees,* Mark A. Abramson and Paul R. Lawrence, editors (Rowman & Littlefield, 2005).

- A large number of specialized publications will be covering your programs. Those publications matter as well. The White House reads *The Washington Post*, but your most engaged stakeholders read the trade press. You will need to deal with both.
- The media are fragmenting as a result of the Internet and new technology. The role of the mainstream media remains important, but the role of bloggers, Twitter, and social media is rising. Pay attention to social media.

## Myths (and Realities) About Career Civil Servants

| Myth | Reality |
|------|---------|
| Careerists are loyal to the previous administration. | • Most careerists check their politics at the door and define their role in terms of the policy process, not the administration's political agenda.<br>• Most careerists see their role as technical, not partisan. |
| Careerists don't work hard. | • Most careerists work extremely hard under tight deadlines and often stressful conditions.<br>• Careerists are "running a marathon;" political appointees are "running a sprint." |
| Careerists are mostly interested in job security. | • Most careerists are motivated by a strong sense of public service, mission dedication, participation in the policy process, and intellectual challenge. |
| Careerists always say no to new ideas. | • Most careerists are not "against" new policy ideas but are sensitive to the various implementation challenges.<br>• Careerists' many years of experience have conditioned them to see change in very pragmatic terms. |
| Careerists want their political bosses to fail. | • Most careerists want their political executives to succeed because they believe in the system and because they want their agencies to succeed. |

From "Getting to Know You: Rules of Engagement for Political Appointees and Career Executives" by Joseph A. Ferrara and Lynn C. Ross. In *Learning the Ropes: Insights for Political Appointees,* Mark A. Abramson and Paul R. Lawrence, editors (Rowman & Littlefield, 2005).

## Get out of your office.

You can learn only so much from briefings and meetings. Get out of the office. Many former agency heads found that undertaking a "listening tour" of field offices and having town hall meetings with employees, and with citizens and users of your agency's services, were very useful. This can be a very enlightening way to learn more about your agency directly from the front line. While doing this can be time consuming, it can create strong links with, and support from, those who are doing the work and interacting with your agency on a day-to-day basis. Meeting them on their turf, not yours, can create a good deal of goodwill, which can help make your job easier.

## Learn the flash points and opportunities.

Every program has hot-button issues that trigger extreme reactions from stakeholder groups. These are often the product of earlier rounds of discussion on an issue and may generate controversy that is disproportionate to the issue at hand. Knowing these flash points beforehand will help you in deciding when to—or if you should—take them on. Actions that look easy may be hard. Alternatively, recent changes may have made easier what used to be difficult, so there may be opportunities as well.

## Begin to assess your senior career staff, but defer judgment.

Federal personnel rules impose what is currently a 120-day period that starts when you take office during which you may not involuntarily reassign members of the Senior Executive Service in your organization. If you bring in a senior political appointee, then the 120-day period starts again for those senior executives reporting to the new appointee.

This law is intended to give you and your senior political staff time to get to know your senior executives before making important personnel decisions. As using them effectively will be critical to your success, this is a good time to start understanding their strengths and weaknesses. An argument they may make against something you want to do may be because they see real problems that are new to you. Or, the argument may be primarily because your approach is new to them. Figuring out which it is will be critical.

The career civil service's ethic is to serve the political leadership of the executive branch. In addition, the senior career staff sees itself as serving the public good. Like you, their oath is to the Constitution and they take it seriously. Odds are they have been with the government, and perhaps even your agency, for decades. The recurring myth that they are loyal to the previous political appointees is almost never true. It is true, however, that they tend to see issues from the agency's perspective. This is both good and bad.

Your senior career staff knows the history of how programs got to where they are today. They understand stakeholder interests and are likely to have credibility with those same stakeholders. They know what has succeeded in the past and what was tried and failed. They will have insights on those failures. They are likely to be quite loyal to the agency. They will be ready to support you when you want to them to.

Your senior career staff is the product of a rough meritocracy. Despite the dysfunctional nature of some of the bureaucracy, careerists at the senior level tend to be highly skilled and very effective within the constraints they face. They can get things done. If they are running large organizations, they know how to manage within the legal and regulatory constraints of federal service. If they are managing budgets, they know how to get resources from OMB and Congress and allocate them to programs in accordance with agency priorities. If they are working with Congress, they know which argument to use with which committee and staff member.

You may want to look at your senior career staff across two dimensions. The first is normally categorized as skills for the job. The skills are standard factors like knowledge, expertise, and the ability to work with people. These are critical to your organization's effectiveness. They are particularly critical because much of getting things done depends on knowledge that only the career people have.

Temperament is the second critical dimension needed for success. Do they display neutral competence? Are they objective and do they give a balanced view of the pros and cons of a strategy? Are they too wedded to the status quo? Finally, do they begin with the outcome and then address the constraints, or is it the other way around? People who begin with the outcome often get more done than those who begin with the constraints.

## Avoid the appearance of unethical behavior.

Ethics matters in government as it does in all walks of life. How it matters differs. The government's ethics rules are about appearances as well as actualities. A government official does not have the latitude to behave in ways that would be well within the private sector's norms. Perhaps more importantly, allegations of ethical improprieties can be used against your policy agenda. You will receive a briefing on government ethics laws and regulations, but here are some useful rules of thumb:

- Don't keep gifts of value. Accept them graciously and pass them to the appropriate agency official.
- Don't mix government and personal travel.
- Don't use someone's private jet for official travel and reimburse the owner for the "full fare equivalent."
- Don't approve your own expense reports. You may have the authority to do so, but give that job to someone else with explicit instructions to question any expense that might be troubling.
- Don't let another organization pay for official travel, even if your staff tells you it is legal.

- Don't get personally involved in contracting. This area has myriad rules that are easy for a newcomer to transgress. Tell your contracting staff what you need and they will work to get it done.
- Don't hire—and don't encourage anybody else in your organization to hire—relatives, no matter how qualified they might be.
- Don't have federal employees do personal services for you or your family, even though they may be eager to do so. Doing so will only spell trouble.

Finally, be careful allowing your staff to do legal things they may want to do for you that might look questionable from the outside. This is not an ethical issue per se, but the media love to do stories on how the taxpayer is being fleeced for an office renovation or expenses such as putting an agency seal on towels or soap. Be sure to meet with your designated agency ethics officer who can help you avoid ethical challenges.

### Learn the politics.

There will be a political dimension to your agency's programs that is likely to be new to you. Learning it will be important to your effectiveness. We mention this last, as you will be more effective if you begin with the program and adjust it to the politics rather than the other way around.

---

# Takeaways

- Learn what your agency's customers want.
- Develop an understanding of your agency's programs and how they achieve the outcomes you want.
- Understand your agency's career workforce.
- Understand that your workforce also may have a large contract workforce.
- Learn what stakeholders want and how they affect your programs.
- Learn how the media affect your programs.
- Get out of your office.
- Learn the flash points and opportunities.
- Begin to assess your senior career staff, but defer judgment.
- Avoid the appearance of unethical behavior.
- Learn the politics.

## CHAPTER THREE

# Act Quickly

# ACT QUICKLY

Developing an understanding of how things work will be one of your early priorities, but you will also need to take some near-term actions. Asking your agency's career staff, customers, key stakeholders, and fellow political appointees questions is the fastest way to learn. Use them all.

G. Edward DeSeve, who served in the Clinton and Obama Administrations in a variety of key roles, recommends that incoming leaders "use existing support functions within their organizations." He says, "Understanding and leveraging existing governance frameworks and processes can speed decisions on presidential priorities."*

### Start to communicate immediately with your new agency's staff with a short, positive message.

Depending on the size of your agency, you may never meet most of your employees, but they will be critical to your success. One of your first acts should be to communicate with them so you can start the relationship on the right foot. You may not know everything you want to do at the beginning, but you still have things to say. Give them a broad-brush picture of what you want to accomplish. Tell them you value their mission and you value their contribution to it. Tell them that part of your approach will be to listen to them to get their insights. Convey a sense of urgency. Don't say what they have been doing is wrong and they need to change, but don't promise that there won't be changes, either.

These early messages are the foundation for future communications which will get into specifics that may involve change or overruling staff recommendations. Use memos, emails, videos, town meetings, blogs, social media, or some combination of these communication vehicles. Use whatever feels most comfortable for you. The key is conveying a positive message at the beginning.

Your early messages should be aspirational, framed in terms of outcomes that matter, and with a sense of urgency and an emphasis on listening as part of your approach. And then, follow through.

### Quickly communicate with agency customers and stakeholders.

It is equally important to start communicating with your customers and key stakeholders. They, too, will be wondering what you and the administration plan to do. A short, positive, aspirational message will help you get started on the right foot. You can then build on it as you implement your program. You may find it necessary to send different messages to different groups. They, of

---

* See *Additional Resources*, page 138.

course, need to be consistent. They should not be detailed because specifics will come later. These messages build a foundation for future conversations.

## Build relationships with your agency's customers and stakeholders.

Getting anything important done in the federal government requires dealing with multiple parties. These include Congress, public interest groups, and industry. These also include other parts of the federal government, other oversight bodies, and the media. It's a long list. It is usually a good idea not to overestimate one's own power as a consequence. Learn who matters on what issue and from what viewpoint, and start to build a relationship with the key players. This will be easier to do before there is a contentious issue and will make that issue easier to resolve.

## Find people in your agency who can help you master processes to meet your needs.

As noted earlier, the Washington environment puts a high premium on process, and how you engage can be as important as what you accomplish. One discounts process at one's peril. Congress has delegated regulatory authority to agencies to make decisions subject to the requirement that they follow certain procedures. Auditors and inspectors general evaluate agencies on whether they follow proper procedures. Criticisms of new policies are sometimes more about following the process than the merits of the new policy.

A key player in managing the "process trains" and keeping things on schedule is your department's executive secretariat. This department coordinates communications internally among key staff, helps orchestrate decision-making timetables on budget and regulatory decisions, and helps prioritize activities and meetings. The executive secretariat often also handles other important, but behind-the-scenes, functions such as records management, Freedom of Information Act requests, and correspondence. Ensuring early on that your department's executive secretariat is highly functional will keep you from having to manage many process-oriented mini-crises that can distract you from the substantive issues facing your agency.

One of the reasons process is so important is that everyone can understand it. Many issues in Washington are complex and different interests put their own spin on them. It is hard for an outsider to figure out the merits of the different policy positions and what is really going on. The public finds it easier to understand that a process was or was not followed. Billion-dollar programs have gotten into trouble over who bought lunch for whom, who met with whom, or who gave what advice. Getting a new policy or program in place will require care in doing it through a process that is viewed as fair, open, and objective.

Find people who can look at what you want to do through a "process" lens and still get things done. On a more mundane level, don't get personally involved in contracting; make sure you have acquisition experts working for you who can get you access to good contractor support quickly. If you are overseeing a regulatory agency, be very careful in any discussions involving those regulations. Rule making follows rigorous procedures that specify how you must make regulatory decisions. Your Office of General Counsel can assist you.

## Find and fix the "ticking bombs."

Out of all the programs your agency is running or planning, some will be "ticking bombs" with a high likelihood of visible failure. Though they are often not predictable, you can learn much about them from talking to your staff, agency customers, and other stakeholders. Your predecessors had an incentive to kick problems to you that could be deferred from their watch. Act quickly to find out what those are and address them. Get ahead of the problems. You may not be able to address all of them, but get to the worst. Have a contingency plan for the others. Some leaders have instituted a "pause and reflect" strategy for programs when they arrive at an agency. If you opt to do that, make sure it is of short duration; the longer the pause, the larger the number of new "ticking bombs."

## Get control of key budget and key agency actions.

Some decisions can't wait until you understand them fully. Move quickly to get control of your budget. Where is the money going? What is it being spent on? What is the process for reprogramming it? Who outside your agency needs to agree (typically OMB and the appropriations committees, but sometimes others)? What is the lead time needed between budget availability and the ability to spend the money? Budgeting, like many government processes, can get quite arcane, but understanding the mechanics can be quite important. An investment in understanding some, but not all, of the arcana can pay off handsomely.

By the same token, your agency is involved in multiple actions, many of which may be extremely important. They were started long before you arrived under policies you may wish to revisit. These might be regulatory actions or some other kind of agency action. Get a handle on the key actions in the pipeline; understand what they are and the consequences of delay.

## Make sure your early political hires align with you.

At the very beginning, you may have very few political appointees. Other than the people you have brought with you, those that are there tend to move on to other jobs after just a few months. There will be a rush to get jobs filled quickly so your agency can move quickly to implement the president's agenda. Some of those jobs need Senate confirmation, which means they will take time to fill. Others that don't require confirmation can be filled immediately. The White House and others will be making suggestions on individuals for jobs. Some of those suggestions will be stronger than others.

The candidates presented to you will demonstrate a wide range of skills that may or may not fit your needs and will have an equally wide range of political supporters. They will be more diverse in their career plans than your existing agency staff. Evaluate them across two dimensions. As with the career staff, the first dimension is matching their skills to the job requirements. The second is that they are aligned with what you want to do. In other words, they will support you rather than a different political constituency.

Many former political appointees have found it more difficult to keep their political staff aligned with their agenda than the career staff. This is particularly important in the early days when there is so much to do with so few people and personnel decisions need to be made very quickly. Keep in mind that once you have taken someone on, you may need White House approval to remove him or her. It is easier to say hello than goodbye.

Finally, your success will depend on forming a joint senior management team that includes both political appointees and senior career staff. When putting together your political staff, think about how the two communities will fit together down the road.

## Get some quick wins.

There will be pressure from the White House and other stakeholders to demonstrate success. As you develop your vision and set priorities, look for examples of efforts already underway in your agency that may reflect them, and hold up those efforts as examples of what you are looking for. This not only gives a sense of progress, but it also provides your staff examples of their peers exemplifying what you are looking for. For example, in the 1990s during the Clinton reinventing government initiative, Vice President Al Gore outlined a set of visionary principles—such as putting customers first and cutting red tape—and then pointed to a team of field employees in the Department of Veterans Affairs that had been quietly working on such an initiative. By highlighting their efforts, he symbolically gave the sense of quick wins and progress, even though the effort had been underway for a number of months before the visionary principles had been announced.

## Get started.

Triage your efforts into: (1) immediate, (2) short term, and (3) long term. Work to keep a balance of your energies across all three time horizons. Your agency will not be standing still while you are figuring out the internal and external environment, deciding on your staffing, and getting a handle on actions that can't wait. You will also be getting engaged in the operations of your agency. Some decisions can be deferred until you can get a better handle on the pros and cons, but many cannot. You will have to get the best advice you can at the time and combine it with your own expertise to start moving forward. Don't let unmade decisions sit and fester; it is often better to make a pretty good decision right away than to wait until the picture is clearer.

---

# Takeaways

- Start to communicate immediately with your new agency's staff with a short, positive message.
- Quickly communicate with agency customers and stakeholders.
- Build relationships with your agency's customers and stakeholders.
- Find people in your agency who can help you master processes to meet your needs.
- Find and fix the "ticking bombs."
- Get control of key budget and key agency actions.
- Make sure your early political hires align with you.
- Get some quick wins.
- Get started.

# CHAPTER FOUR

## Develop a Vision and a Focused Agenda

# DEVELOP A VISION AND A FOCUSED AGENDA

You may have come to your agency to manage an ongoing operation that works reasonably well following traditional processes. You may have come to help your agency deliver new programs. You may have the goal of completely transforming your agency and redefining its mission.

Your efforts at your agency may be an integral part of the administration's core agenda with regular senior-level direction from the White House. Or, you may find that it is almost completely up to you to decide what your agency priorities should be. Whatever your situation, you will want to convey your overall vision but concentrate on a few key priorities.

Your vision can inspire your colleagues, workforce, and constituents to think and act creatively in carrying out your strategic priorities in the context of your agency's mission. As Beth Noveck and Stefaan G. Verhulst, both of the Governance Lab at New York University, wrote, "Innovation can be a critical tool for the next administration to achieve presidential priorities and improve government operations."*

**Develop a vision for your agency with input from your political and career staff, but make sure it is your own.**

A vision gives the big picture view of where you want to take your agency. It should clearly describe the broad outcomes you want to have accomplished when you leave the agency. State your vision simply and do not weigh it down with too many adjectives or dependent clauses. It needs to be aligned with your agency's core values and programs. It needs to be realistic, but it also needs to be aspirational and push your agency beyond what it is achieving today. It should make sense to the agency's customers. Ideally, it will give your employees a line of sight between what they do in their jobs and the vision.

The administration taking office in 2017 will be the first to benefit from a law passed in 2010 that creates a new lever for incoming agency leaders to embed their new visions into the institutional processes of their agencies. The Government Performance and Results Modernization Act requires agencies to refresh their strategic plans at the beginning of each new administration and deliver those plans to Congress along with their first budget in the subsequent year. Agencies must also align their annual operating plan (technically called the "agency performance plan") with the goals in the new strategic plan. Many agencies also tie their executives' personal performance agreements to their progress of these plans. This gives you a mechanism and a set of processes to influence action on the vision and priorities important to you and the new administration.

Test your vision against the administration's agenda and your political and senior career staff, but make sure it is yours. Your career staff can tell

---

* See *Additional Resources,* page 138.

you how what you say may be heard, what words are "loaded," and how your vision compares to what has been tried in the past.

Work with your senior political and career staff in crafting the vision, but don't let a committee write it. Committees add adjectives and clauses as they labor to cover all the contingencies. You want something that inspires, not something exhaustive. Good visions tell a story in which people can see themselves.

## Convey a sense of urgency.

If your vision is centered on outcomes that matter, it is important to get there sooner rather than later. The tendency in Washington is for complexity, scale, and responsibility diffusion, which slows things down. If you don't convey a sense of urgency, your agency may never get there.

## Communicate the vision.

An effective vision drives behavior. It cannot simply be a slogan on a wall or a new brochure. It needs to be real. You will need to communicate the vision regularly. You will need stories that illustrate what it means. Your agency will need to have short-term objectives that get it closer to that vision.

You will need a strategy to convey the vision to more than your immediate staff. They have a good idea of what you are looking for, but there are hundreds, perhaps thousands, of others who lack that advantage. Talking about what you want to achieve and why it matters will be important. You can supplement your personal efforts with staff's efforts to help with written material and with choosing the right media venues. You may even want to start your own blog and participate in social media.

Communicating your vision will be critical to keeping your agency on track and should be a priority. It will take a continuous effort to communicate to the rank and file what you want to do and why it matters in a way that enables them to see themselves in the picture. The more you can convey what you want in terms that make sense to them, the more effective your organization will be. It is almost impossible to over-communicate. So many voices talk to them that even your voice will have trouble getting through. The same is true of your key stakeholders. Keep the message simple and in terms that matter to your agency's customers, and repeat it over and over again. Make sure the message makes sense in the larger context of what the administration wants to deliver.

## Harness agency plans to your new vision.

The agency's strategic and tactical plans will need to be adjusted to reflect your new vision. There may be budget implications as well. Task your staff with making those changes and briefing you quarterly on their progress.

Do not get too engaged in the details, but use the meetings to assess whether the agency is moving in the right direction overall. Use the agency's existing planning mechanisms rather than developing new ones.

## In alignment with your agency's priority goals (see Chapter Six), select a few priorities where you can personally make a difference.

You have more to get done than you can get done. Your agency faces a large number of pressing issues calling for your attention. Many of them you know about and care about because that is what made you want to take this job in the first place. You can't do them all, and the more you spread your energies, the less you will get done. When everything is a priority, nothing is a priority. You will need to decide on a few big things that you want to accomplish during your tenure. Pick those that matter and are possible. Tie them to your vision.

You may want to get up every morning and go through a mental checklist of how your actions that day will advance these big things. This does not mean that you ignore everything else your agency does, but it does mean that you keep personally focused on the big things.

Keep your goals in outcome terms and revisit them regularly. Keep asking yourself:
- What does success look like?
- What do I want to achieve?
- What outputs or milestones do I need to achieve this month to move toward one of the outcomes?
- Am I being pulled off course by the crisis of the moment?

You should regularly look up and make sure you are still going in the right direction.

## Develop a strategy for your top priorities in consultation with both political and career staff.

An effective strategy will combine what you and your fellow political appointees know and want to do with your agency's expertise and resources. Developing that strategy will take a joint effort of the two communities. Your career staff has a huge amount of knowledge and experience that you will need. Many of them have dedicated their careers to the programs you now lead, but they cannot get things done without your political leadership. Each community needs the other to get it done.

Listen to the career staff, but weigh their advice carefully. They may feel more limited in their options than you or your political staff. Combining the two viewpoints will lead to a better result. You can learn much from discussions around some basic questions:
- What has been tried before that was similar to what I am proposing?

## Now What?

"The challenge in Washington, I began to realize, was not getting the job, but figuring out what to do with it."

– David Kessler, former Commissioner,
Food and Drug Administration

From *A Question of Intent: A Great American Battle with a Deadly Industry* by David Kessler (New York: PublicAffairs, 2001).

- Why did it work or not work and how do I know?
- What are the legal and regulatory constraints? If your staff tells you something is illegal or contrary to regulation, get them to show you exactly where it is written in law or regulation. There is a lot of lore within the government about what is legal or illegal that is more tradition than fact. Probe to make sure this is not tradition or legal interpretation that could be interpreted in some other way. But assess whether an incorrect legal argument is fronting for a valid policy or stakeholder issue.
- Who cares about what we are doing? What do they want? Will they weigh in and try to affect the outcome? In what way? How do we know? How should we respond?

### Make sure there is a person accountable for implementing each of your priorities.

At the broadest level, a strategy requires a goal and a plan to get there. That plan includes the basics like putting someone in charge, making sure resources are available and managed, and following up periodically to make sure progress is being made. That strategy should place a particular emphasis on stakeholder management and be designed to adjust to contingencies.

The strategy should provide you and your agency with a roadmap to successfully negotiate a path through all the diverse interests that make Washington so difficult. An effective strategy leverages supporters and neutralizes adversaries. Resist the temptation to concentrate only on supporters. Concentrate on groups who disagree with you or are neutral. It is often more important to pay more attention to those who disagree with you than those who agree. The nature of Washington is such that it is easier to stop something new than it is to do something new, and neutrals don't always stay neutral.

As noted earlier, your strategy to achieve your top priorities will be a product of the insights from your political staff as well as the knowledge and experience from your career staff. The combination of political knowledge and agency experience will give you a far stronger approach than either could on its own. Although you will want to keep some distance from the mechanics of executing a strategy, you will want to make sure that there are good answers to the following questions:

- Who will be in charge and accountable for delivery? Why does that person have the qualifications to do this job? Does that person have control of program resources or is he or she dependent on others in my organization?
- What resources will be needed in dollars and staffing? You will need to make sure resources are set aside and fenced off to support the program. Will the fence hold or will the next priority bleed off the resources? You don't want to fall into the trap of your agency always pursuing the next better idea before it finishes the last one.
- How much of my personal time will be needed and in what ways?

Finally, your strategy should plan for the inevitable surprises. No important project unfolds as planned in this environment. Stakeholders weigh in on objectives and force adjustments. Congress does not always appropriate all the necessary funds. Contract award dates slip. Being flexible and always having a "plan B" are key ingredients of success. That said, there may come a time when plan B is so far from the original goal that it is better to cancel and move on. Thinking through that contingency at the beginning is a useful, albeit depressing, exercise. Some deals are worse than no deal, but that can be harder to discern months later after major resources have been spent in the heat of the moment.

### Make sure there is an effective governance framework for your top priorities.

Big initiatives cross organizational lines or depend on other initiatives for success. Successful big initiatives depend on sound program management, but they also depend on clarity about who makes decisions on what. Your top priorities will be no exception. You not only need to have a sound strategy and someone strong in charge of execution, but you also need to ensure that the program management operates in a governance framework that will allow it to succeed. Some of this can be handled by staying actively engaged, but you will find it easier if there is a clear process for raising and resolving problems that does not require your personal attention.

We have seen many political appointees differ on the question of on how many issues they should focus. One former agency head received advice from several former appointees to just select a couple of issues and focus on those items. She chose instead to focus on a cluster of activities aimed at improving the entire organization. Some of the best appointees have "tiered goals"—more like concentric circles—where they focus on a few key priorities that everyone knows, with additional, more targeted goals in specific areas that they support but do not engage with on a daily basis.

Different strategies can work well in different situations. The key is consistent and ongoing focus. This ongoing focus includes what one executive calls "relentless follow-up." Thus, the most important factor in having an impact on your organization is continued focus—whether it be on a limited or a larger number of items.

### Relentlessly follow up.

The daily pressures on your time and attention will make it hard to concentrate on those few items that will be your most important legacy. Your agency will be buffeted by many issues that risk displacing your key priorities and pushing them to the back burner. Find a way to always keep your top priorities in front of you. Regularly follow up with those tasked with implementing the strategy for your highest priorities. Probe. People tend to put the best face on what the boss wants. Get second opinions and compare them to the internal reports. You want a realistic, not an optimistic, picture. You may want to make your top priorities a topic at every staff meeting.

Track measurable milestones, monitor key stakeholder relationships, and watch for the unpleasant surprise. Don't let the urgent drive out the important, and don't succumb to the tyranny of the many. Concentrating on what matters most will help you deliver on what matters most.

Your staff, particularly your senior staff, may need regular reminders of what is important. Follow up with them so they stay focused on your priorities. Just as you will wake up every morning thinking about how to make progress on the things that matter most to you, you want them to wake up every morning thinking the same.

---

# Takeaways

- Develop a vision for your agency with input from your political and career staff, but make sure it is your own.
- Convey a sense of urgency.
- Communicate the vision.
- Harness agency plans to your new vision.
- In alignment with your agency's priority goals (see Chapter Six), select a few priorities where you can personally make a difference.
- Develop a strategy for your top priorities in consultation with both political and career staff.
- Make sure there is a person accountable for implementing each of your priorities.
- Make sure there is an effective governance framework for your top priorities.
- Relentlessly follow up.

## CHAPTER FIVE

# Assemble Your Leadership Team

# ASSEMBLE YOUR LEADERSHIP TEAM

Your team needs to be able to effectively develop and implement all your agency's programs, not just your top priorities. Your programs will cross many interests. The team will need to work effectively with multiple stakeholders on both the programmatic and political dimensions. The team will need to address a complex external environment, a complex internal environment, tight resource constraints, and cumbersome processes.

Agencies are too complicated to be managed at a distance by a small cadre of political appointees developing a strategy and then directing a larger body of career staff to execute against that strategy. Such an approach will run into obstacles that could have been avoided with a wider initial conversation between your political staff and career staff. It needs to be a joint effort.

A 2015 report by Douglas Brook, former senior official in the George H.W. Bush and George W. Bush Administrations, and Maureen Hartney says that a critical success factor for moving quickly to implement key administration priorities is to create: "Joint executive management teams at the department and agency level that quickly coalesce and include both political and career leaders" in order to create shared expectations and objectives. Creating shared accountability increases your chances for success.*

### Leverage the senior career staff: Find out to whom you should listen and on what.

Your agency is large and complex, with all the vices of a large bureaucracy. It has a cadre of senior career managers who are ready and able to get that large bureaucracy to do what you want it to do. Those senior career managers support your agency's mission and recognize that they need political leadership to achieve it. Those senior managers will be critical to your success, but they are also part of the same bureaucracy.

The senior career managers overseeing this bureaucracy are skilled at getting it to move forward, although their approaches may sometimes stick too closely to the traditional. The vehicle may be obsolete, but they know how to drive it. You will find many people in your agency at both senior and lower levels that have an entrepreneurial bent. Unlike the private sector entrepreneur who pursues profit, these government entrepreneurs pursue program results or transformation. They care about the mission and know how to get the larger organization to move in a desired direction. Many have good ideas on how to improve service delivery that will assist you in your own agenda. Your senior leadership team can help you leverage this entrepreneurial energy as well as get the bureaucratic behemoth you now manage to move in the right direction.

However, you may need different skills from those your agency needed in the past. You may find some of your staff too wedded to the status quo and

---

* See *Additional Resources,* page 138.

too quick to explain why the way things work is the way things should be. Your most important skill will be figuring out to whom you should listen and on what. When some people tell you not to take a course of action, they may be warning you against very real dangers. When others warn you against a course of action, they may simply be embracing traditional ways of operating.

You will need to figure out who are the former and who are the latter. Further, you will find that one person has good insights in one area and poor ones in another. One may be good on the politics but weak on program realities. One may be strong on program issues but oblivious to the political ramifications. Leveraging the right strengths from the right people leads to success. Not listening at all or listening to the wrong people on the wrong issues risks failure.

## Hire senior political staff with the right political talents.

Your career staff are largely in place, but they will be less effective without political leadership. Selecting your political appointees will be among your most important decisions. It often requires approval from the White House. Your selections will need to meet the needs of both you and the White House. Most of the selection criteria will be specific to your agency and the job, but some are more general in nature.

- Choose appointees who have the talents and existing relationships to work effectively with political interests outside your agency and with your stakeholders. They will be particularly important in working with your agency's key constituencies.
- Choose appointees who have the technical and people skills needed for the specific job. You will be under pressure to employ political staff that the administration likes for various reasons. Not all candidates have the right skills for your needs. Match skills to needs.
- Choose appointees who have energy and are committed to your agenda. They should see the larger picture and commit to sticking around for a while. Many appointees have a short time horizon for a job. It needs to be long enough to meet your needs.
- Finally, at the risk of being indelicate, choose appointees who will support you over other political interests. Most political appointments involve some balancing of different political interests. Different wings of the party, different geographic regions, and different congressional support all come into play. You will need political staff that are loyal to you and your agenda first.

The right mix of political staff will be crucial to achieving your goals.

## Blend political and career staff: Leverage their different strengths.

Your success will depend on your ability to build an effective senior management team to carry out your, and the administration's, agenda. It will need

# Rules of Engagement for Political Appointees

| Rule | Illustration |
|------|-------------|
| Engage the career staff and listen to their advice—even if you don't ultimately heed it. | • Involve the career staff in agency deliberations.<br>• Actively solicit their analysis and recommendations. |
| Show the career staff that you respect them. | • Read your careerists' résumés.<br>• Understand their skills and what they bring to the table.<br>• Make it clear that you are the decision maker, but treat them as partners. |
| Spend some time learning the details. | • Ask lots of questions—particularly as you enter office.<br>• Find out why some initiatives have worked and others haven't.<br>• Know the details to give you stronger credibility within the agency and improve the chances of achieving your agenda. |
| Have a clear and limited set of objectives. | • Motivate the career staff with ambitious but achievable objectives.<br>• Make sure the careerists know where you're going.<br>• Make sure you know where you're going. |
| Be willing to compromise and admit mistakes. | • Realize that sometimes you have to give a little to gain a little.<br>• Be strong but pragmatic.<br>• Take responsibility for your mistakes. |
| Don't forget about the organization. | • Pay attention to organizational stewardship.<br>• Take on bureaucratic and administrative problems within the agency.<br>• Make an effort to attend job fairs and new employee orientation events.<br>• Don't shy away from tough human resource management issues. |
| Communicate, communicate, communicate. | • Constantly communicate your goals.<br>• Constantly give the career staff feedback about ongoing agency deliberations.<br>• Make sure that the staff understand why decisions have been made.<br>• Give the staff feedback on their performance. |

From "Getting to Know You: Rules of Engagement for Political Appointees and Career Executives" by Joseph A. Ferrara and Lynn C. Ross. In *Learning the Ropes: Insights for Political Appointees,* Mark A. Abramson and Paul R. Lawrence, editors (Rowman & Littlefield, 2005).

to be a blend of senior political and career staff working together. It should not be an inner circle of political appointees who then communicate with the career staff. That road leads to failure, as programs with major flaws not visible to the political staff get started and later need to be adjusted or, worse, fail. It is better to fix the problems internally as part of the design than to fix them publicly as part of a redesign.

Political appointees often begin their tenure with reservations about the career staff. Invariably, they leave government service with a high opinion of the majority of the career staff they have worked with, lauding their ability, knowledge, work ethic, and integrity. Interestingly, career staff say the same kinds of things about the political appointees they have served under when surveyed after the fact.

That said, what is true of the average is not true for all. You need to build a team that delivers on your agenda. That means you need people committed to the mission and with the right skills for their job, not some other job. They also need to be able to work together and resolve the inevitable conflicts.

Three geniuses who cannot work together may be worse than three solid people who can. You will need to assess your senior career staff as individuals and decide whether they are the right fit for where you want to go or if they might best support the government somewhere else. Consult with your human resources staff if you want to move people, as process is particularly difficult in the personnel arena.

### Recognize that political appointees and careerists have different roles and responsibilities.

Despite having stressed the importance of a joint political/career team, it is worth emphasizing that each is part of a distinct community. The two communities have different roles that need to fit together well for success.

Careerists tend to manage down and concentrate more on service delivery. Politicals tend to manage up and out and work on managing the stakeholders and the message. The political community is part of an administration that will last four to eight years and then move on. Its members bring innovation, a new agenda, and the political connections to bring it about. They usually make or advocate policy. They are subject to different personnel rules and will be involved in political activities that are forbidden to career employees.

The career workforce tends to have a longer time horizon with the federal government, although the old lifetime employment model appears to be declining. The career workforce brings continuity and the operational skills to ensure programs are carried on from prior administrations or beyond the current one. It tends to be more the policy implementer than the maker. It is subject to different personnel rules and cannot be involved in political activity.

## The Role of the Careerist

Careerists want to feel like they are contributing to the mission of their organizations. If political managers cut them out of processes or if their advice is rarely sought, they suffer from a sort of professional identity crisis. Such an identity crisis negatively affects their job satisfaction and motivation. Ultimately, the productivity and the effectiveness of the organization will be negatively affected, too.

Careerists are the institutional memory of American public administration.... They draw the policy maps that connect the past, present, and future. They are the keepers of the institutional "lore" and can tell political appointees the stories that explain what has and hasn't worked before. As Richard Neustadt once wrote, "What makes lore invaluable is the sad fact that no institutional sources of memory exist as substitutes, save patchily, by happenstance, at higher executive levels of American government. Lore is almost all there is. Without it, available documentation tends to be ambiguous, misleading, or perverse."

From "Getting to Know You: Rules of Engagement for Political Appointees and Career Executives" by Joseph A. Ferrara and Lynn C. Ross. In *Learning the Ropes: Insights for Political Appointees,* Mark A. Abramson and Paul R. Lawrence, editors (Rowman & Littlefield, 2005).

## Be careful how you blend the political and career jobs.

To a large degree, political and career jobs will be defined before you arrive. Political jobs tend to be reserved for senior policy makers and their immediate support staff, or for positions in which the administration conveys its views to the public. Career jobs tend to be more operational, or reserved to ensure the public's confidence in the impartiality of the government.

Placing political appointees in operational jobs carries some risks. If you place a political appointee between career employees in an operational management chain, you risk reducing the operational efficiency of your organization. The careerists will be inclined to look for a political "sign off" or feel the need to clear actions at a higher level. The appointee is like a "circuit breaker" in your management accountability chain that will regularly have to be reset.

This has nothing to do with the skills of the politicals and everything to do with organizational culture. It can be overcome, but it needs to be addressed at the beginning. A simple example is when a career executive manages a national program but regional operations for that program have been placed under a political appointee. Expect simple operational decisions to come back to your senior political staff for resolution, taking time away from your real agenda and slowing your agency's reaction time. Unless you address this up front, you or your senior staff will be refereeing operational disputes.

In the long run, this can also have an impact on your legacy. One of the virtues of the career bureaucracy is continuity. What begins under you is more likely to continue when careerists run it. If the program is controversial, it has

# Differences Between Political Appointees and Career Civil Servants*

| Factor | Political appointees | Careerists |
|---|---|---|
| Role perception | • "Determine the nation's business" <br>• Focused on achieving policy outcomes | • "Do the nation's business" <br>• Focused on ensuring a fair, open, and sound decision process |
| Partisanship | • Affiliated with a political party <br>• Serve a particular president | • Nonpartisan on the job <br>• Serve various presidents |
| Professional experience | • Often a mix of government, academic, and private sector | • Government has been their main career |
| Tenure of service | • Come in and go out <br>• Average about two years in their positions, about four years in their agency, and about nine years of government service | • In for the long term <br>• Senior executives average six years in their SES position and more than 23 years in government service** |
| Time perspective | • Tend to have a shorter-term outlook | • Tend to have a longer-term outlook |

* From "Getting to Know You: Rules of Engagement for Political Appointees and Career Executives" by Joseph A. Ferrara and Lynn C. Ross. In *Learning the Ropes: Insights for Political Appointees,* Mark A. Abramson and Paul R. Lawrence, editors (Rowman & Littlefield, 2005).

** From *Mission-Driven Mobility: Strengthening Our Government Through a Mobile Leadership Corps,* Partnership for Public Service, February 2012

a reduced likelihood of continuing if it is under the direct management of a political appointee. You may want to have politicals in operational jobs as you get started, but at some point you will want to move careerists into those jobs for your legacy's sake.

## Keep "political appointees only" meetings rare and reserve them for political matters.

Your effectiveness in getting your agency to do what you want it to do will depend on your ability to build an effective joint political/career team. Your staff meetings should be joint, as should most of the meetings involving your agency's management. Nonetheless, you will find that you occasionally need to meet separately with your political staff on political issues. Such meetings might cover political strategy or campaigns. These are necessary and the careerists should not be there. However, you will have more success running your agency if the two communities regularly work together in policy development and implementation.

## Put it all together and decide on whom to depend and for what.

Step one in harnessing the power of the career bureaucracy is figuring out to whom you should listen and on what. But that is only step one. The more critical step is figuring out on whom to depend and for what. This applies to both the career and political side of your organization. You will find most of your career staff have the right combination of knowledge and inclination to support your agenda. Some may not be in the best positions to exploit the full force of their talents and need to move to new positions. Others may not be a good fit for what you want to accomplish and need to move as well.

Your success will depend on how well you put together this joint political/career team to deliver on your agenda. Some of this will be matching skills to the job, but some of this will be finding the right chemistry between your politicals and careerists. If you have a good team that works well together, you can get it done.

## Don't reorganize your agency.

One last thought: Reorganize only as a last resort. Government reorganizations consume enormous resources, always take much longer than planned, and focus energies internally at the expense of the mission. If you do reorganize, make sure you do it quickly, have the right career staff in charge, and don't try to fix too many problems at once. Otherwise the process takes over, and it is easy to lose a year or more to a reorganization initiative.

---

# Takeaways

- Leverage the senior career staff: Find out to whom you should listen and on what.
- Hire senior political staff with the right political talents.
- Blend political and career staff: Leverage their different strengths.
- Recognize that political appointees and careerists have different roles and responsibilities.
- Be careful how you blend the political and career jobs.
- Keep "political appointees only" meetings rare and reserve them for political matters.
- Put it all together and decide on whom to depend and for what.
- Don't reorganize your agency.

## CHAPTER SIX

# Deliver Results

# DELIVER RESULTS

Your main thing will be keeping "the main thing" as your main thing, as one former federal agency head remarked. Your vision, agenda, and leadership team will be pulled in multiple directions, and the more directions you pursue, the harder it will be to deliver any results.

A former deputy secretary divided issues crossing his desk into three buckets and consciously ensured an appropriate balance among them to effectively deliver expected results:

- The first bucket is comprised of new initiatives—reforming the tax code, standing up a new poverty program, launching a food safety education campaign, a "cyber sprint" to reduce vulnerabilities, etc. These might be self-generated or imposed by the White House or the Office of Management and Budget. These may be initially small and time-intensive activities, but with some discretion over their progress.
- The second bucket is comprised of the day-to-day operations of the agency's mission—air traffic control, processing patents, collecting employment statistics, inspecting meat plants, etc. This is where the majority of your agency's staff will be focused. Oftentimes, these are run efficiently and effectively by career staff and will likely not require a great deal of your personal time.
- The third bucket is unanticipated events—like the BP oil spill, an especially vicious hurricane, a pandemic outbreak, a scandal in another agency where "fixes" suddenly affect your agency, etc. These cannot be planned for but need to be expected. They oftentimes have the capacity to consume a large part of your time and energy.

Having a clear vision and priorities helps, even when you're buffeted by many other demands.

## Leverage existing processes, including strategic reviews.

Avoid the temptation to start by creating your own decision-making processes or new operating committees. Conduct a review of what processes and committees are already in place. Typically, there are decision processes such as strategic planning, budgeting, and performance management; and there are operating processes such as contracting, grants, and personnel. Many of these have statutory roots and may not be easily susceptible to change.

Determine if the processes work and add value, and if so, use them. It will take less time and energy to leverage what is there than to create new ones. For example, if you want an external advisory body, see if one already exists that you can adapt. Because of existing open government laws, creating a new one could take up to a year.

In recent years, agencies have created regular data-driven review forums (e.g., HUD-Stat and the deputy secretary of Veterans Affairs' monthly performance reviews) to convene agency leaders around targeted priority goals to assess progress and solve problems. Agencies also hold annual strategic reviews to assess progress on broad objectives and resources needed to ensure progress in the future.

## Make sure agency operations are running effectively.

You cannot ignore the need for the agency to be managed. You will have a more than full-time job managing political and stakeholder relationships, your own priorities, and the various crises that will occur during your tenure. Management is a difficult discipline that requires a set of rare skills. The federal government also offers a manager unique challenges because it puts such a high premium on adherence to process and has multiple points where external organizations (e.g., Congress or OMB) can intervene.

You will need someone, or perhaps several people, with the right management skills, including an ability to manage in the federal government "ecosystem." We cannot emphasize enough that effective management depends on a high degree of skill and it will be critical to get people who have those skills. Don't go for people who just have the right idea on the policy. This is a different skill from getting that policy implemented.

One effective model is to pair a political appointee with a career deputy to manage day-to-day operations, but the effectiveness of that model depends on how well that deputy works with your political appointee and how often you would need to get engaged. Whatever approach you take, make sure you have skilled managers overseeing agency operations.

## Maintain a results-oriented climate and a sense of urgency.

Maintaining a results-oriented climate in your agency will be important to mission success and may require you to overcome two tendencies within the bureaucracy. First, the federal government puts a high value on process, but it has multiple organizations establishing and overseeing these processes. The federal government, however, has poor methods for resolving the inevitable contradictions resulting from these overlapping processes. Worse, the established processes are buffeted by external pressures from Congress, OMB, and other stakeholders who will impose reporting, reducing or changing budgets, and adding extra requirements.

Second, individuals tend to be rewarded more for process adherence than for program results. There are few individual financial rewards for mission success, and penalties for mission failure tend to be modest as well. Many people motivated to achieve the mission work in spite of the incentives, but many go with the flow.

You can overcome these two factors by maintaining a climate that frames issues around how they help or hinder achieving the agency's mission. You can require that the right issues be handled at the right level. You can make sure that there is a governance framework around your programs that at least gets the basics right: authority and accountability in the same place, people in charge of their programs having control over the budgets to deliver those programs, clarity on who can make what decisions, and a clear and quick process for raising and resolving issues.

### Make sure your mission-support executives (chief financial, acquisition, information, and human capital officers, as well as the general counsel) are focused on program results, not their fiefdoms.

You will depend on your program managers for program results, but they will be dependent on other support organizations to deliver. Someone needs to manage the supporting people, technology, contracts, and financials. You should not be personally involved in these questions, but you will want to make sure that you have strong people in charge of these areas and that they can work together to support the programs. This is a special case of the discussion just above, but worth emphasizing in its own right.

Unfortunately, these different professional communities are often better at dictating what they want the rest of the agency to do for them rather than finding a joint strategy to support the larger mission. The financial community will tell you it needs a clean audit. The acquisition community will stress the need for good contract oversight. The information technology community will stress the importance of a standard infrastructure. The human capital community will stress the need for a human capital plan. And the attorneys will stress the need for legal sufficiency.

All of these are important, but they only matter in the context of your mission. You cannot afford to spend time refereeing disputes about whether a financial computer system falls under the financial area or information technology. It is both. You can tell the various areas' leadership that you expect them to work together and the test of success is whether the agency mission succeeds. Your programs need the legally sufficient joint product of technology, contracting, finance, and human resources, not the clash of each community's independent view.

### Keep the discussion on evidence-based measurable results.

The trend in recent decades has been to move more of the government conversation to the results achieved rather than the resources expended. Not all constituencies embrace this approach and any discussion of results is open to spin. Nonetheless, an ongoing concentration on results has value beyond the ideas of good government, particularly as the American people have become less trusting of the government. Focusing on results helps your agency concentrate on the things that matter.

In recent years, there has also been an emphasis on evidence-based approaches, and many of these are embedded into existing programs, mostly on the domestic side of government. For example, data-driven analyses have contributed to reductions in crime and recidivism, and recent legislation has created demonstration pilots to better coordinate disability activities across the federal government based on what works. Several agencies have created "what works" clearinghouses of program evaluation studies on different programmatic interventions in areas such as education, employment, and law enforcement. Because many of these "what works" initiatives focus on creating measurable results, they have bipartisan appeal.

Finally, using measurable results gives you the moral high ground in debates with critics and can help you in the court of public opinion. Keep yourself and your agency focused on measurable results.

---

## Takeaways

- Leverage existing processes, including strategic reviews.
- Make sure agency operations are running effectively.
- Maintain a results-oriented climate and a sense of urgency.
- Make sure your mission-support executives (chief financial, acquisition, information, and human capital officers, as well as the general counsel) are focused on program results, not their fiefdoms.
- Keep the discussion on evidence-based measurable results.

## CHAPTER SEVEN

# Manage Your Environment

# MANAGE YOUR ENVIRONMENT

First, pace yourself. You can't do it all in the first 100 days. Your agency needs leadership more than it needs you to work long hours. You will find that your biggest impact will come through your ability to maintain a focus on your vision for the agency and on your stakeholders, to keep your agency focused on your top priorities, and to manage crises that are sure to come up during your tenure.

Second, your vision needs constant repetition. You need to maintain your relationship with key stakeholders so there is a good foundation for resolving the inevitable issues. You cannot allow the many urgent crises to push your program priorities to the back burner. You need to keep crises from taking all of your time and the agency's.

Third, you must constantly be aware of all your stakeholders and pro-actively manage your environment.

In a 2016 report on the importance of taking an enterprise-wide view of the governmental environment, Jane Fountain, University of Massachusetts at Amherst, writes that government increasingly "operates across boundaries and engages in coordinated, cross-agency collaboration to address many of the nation's complex problems." She advises that: "Leaders will accelerate achievement of the president's priorities if they understand and use multi-agency initiatives and integrated management as key levers to accomplish policy goals and prevent operational failures."*

### Manage the politics.

One of your most important roles will be the political dimension of managing your agency. We will not be so presumptuous as to tell you how to do this. To put it simply, you must stay on top of the political issues. You must be careful in delegating political issues to your political staff. Keep a wide gap between political activities and your career staff. Also, keep a wide gap between political and agency activities.

### Manage the stakeholder relationships, but save your personal time for the most important ones.

Your agency has long-standing relationships with the White House, the Office of Management and Budget, Congress, customers, industry, oversight bodies, and the media. These relationships transcend any individual program or decision.

Managing these relationships will be one of your most important roles. In some cases you will want to get personally involved. In other cases it will work better if your staff does it. Managing stakeholder relationships is a bit like

---

\* See *Additional Resources*, page 138.

business world negotiations, which ensure that senior executives are brought in only at the appropriate time. Your personal involvement should be reserved for the most important issues or the most senior stakeholders. Make sure your subordinates are appropriately involved and step in as needed.

### Meet regularly with your senior political/career management team on agency programs.

You are the head of a large agency that needs to be well managed. Most of this will be done by your senior management team. Meet regularly with them, making sure they are on top of what matters to the agency, not just what matters to you. This will help keep a secondary problem from turning into a full-fledged crisis and requiring your personal time. Make sure people who have the right training, experience, and aptitude are in charge of day-to-day management. The best policies in the world are worthless if the agency implementing them is adrift.

### Don't take too long to fill important jobs or let key decisions slip.

Decisions need to be made in a timely manner because the consequences of making no decision are often worse than choosing the less-than-perfect option. Management slots need to be filled rather than left empty for months or even years, as is too often the case. Budgets have time limits on their availability and need to be allocated to programs early enough in the year so the money can be spent wisely—not "dumped" into an available program weeks before the money expires. Leaders with only policy expertise need deputies who are good at management, and they must work well with and support the deputies in making the regular hard decisions to keep policy implementation on track.

### Empower your team, stay current with what they are doing, and focus on the big picture.

You are here to run an agency, not do projects. You have built a joint political/career team. You have ensured that the right people are in the right jobs. Empower them to deliver on the program. Follow up regularly on the progress.

Conserve your energy for what really matters. You may have to work directly with Congress. You may have to resolve disputes between different parts of your agency. You may need to engage with the White House. You may even have to engage on specifics with OMB, which over the past few presidencies has become increasingly involved in internal agency operations. Think of yourself as an orchestra conductor, not one of the musicians.

### Reward innovation, collaboration, and success.

The federal government's incentive system puts too much weight on process and not enough weight on results, and it tends to be more top-down than collaborative. Process is a necessary element of program management, but alone it is not sufficient. Innovation is an important means to deal with shrinking budgets.

Organizations throughout the world increase their effectiveness through collaboration. By collaborating we are not invoking altruism and the value of working together for the common good. Appeals to altruism are of limited value. Appealing to the self-interest of different links in a chain has enormous value. Effective collaboration depends on pursuing pragmatic policies such that the various participants individually gain from the collaboration. Find ways to reward innovation, collaboration, and results. There are already enough incentives to follow existing procedures.

### Manage the crises. Plan for unpleasant surprises and act quickly when they happen.

No matter how effective you are, how strong your team is, or how popular your programs are, something will go badly on your watch. All you can do is take steps to find out about those ticking bombs, take steps to avoid them before they go off, and be ready to address the issues when they do. Make your people think the unthinkable and prepare contingency plans. When the surprise happens, it will probably be something that wasn't planned for, but the anticipatory effort will make your agency better prepared.

When—not if—something does go wrong, the rules are straightforward. Act quickly to fix or mitigate the problem. Tell the public what happened and what you are doing about it. Do not try to cover it up. Cover-ups always fail and often cause more damage to your credibility than the original problem. Get information out quickly as you learn it. Only give out information that you know to be accurate. If you don't know, say you don't know. Yes, you may be criticized for not being on top of the situation, but it is worse to be attacked later for sending out misinformation.

### Manage yourself. Don't let your calendar manage you.

Your priorities will come from the president and the White House, but you have some latitude. To frame it perhaps too baldly, you have the opportunity to make a big difference on a few things or no difference on a great many things. Many of your predecessors have found that they could get things done by focusing on a few priorities and not letting themselves be distracted—and there are many distractions. Your agency faces a great many problems. Addressing those problems crosses many diverse interests. Solutions tend to cross the boundaries between agencies, interest groups, and the private sector. Getting anything important done is difficult and will require your undivided attention.

Your calendar and in-box will be your worst enemies. Every day someone will want you to give a speech. Every day there will be too many meetings. Every day there will be too many documents to read and sign. Find ways to make those demands part of someone else's day so you can concentrate on what really matters. Delegate so you can concentrate.

### Find people who will tell you the truth. Listen to them.

It is human nature to tell the boss what he or she wants to hear. You will have a communications organization working hard to put everything you do in the best possible light. You will have people coming to meet with you who want your agency to take some action. They, too, will tend to tell you what they think you want to hear. Much of the political establishment will be doing the same. Congressional oversight hearings might seem to be an antidote to this, but they are more often exercises in political theater than an attempt to convey a realistic picture of what is really going on.

Find people who will speak straight to you and tell you what you should worry about. Family and friends can be invaluable for this, but they often are not as close to the issues that matter for your agency as you might need. Find ways to talk to frontline employees as well as customers and citizens that deal directly with your agency. You may be able to learn more in five minutes from a real customer than in any status briefing.

### Embed your legacy in the career bureaucracy, not your political subordinates.

Programs and policies that last longer than a single administration depend on at least some degree of consensus between the two political parties and the executive and legislative branches. You are best positioned to determine if your legacy meets this political test and can outlast your tenure. You should also embed your programs in the hands of your career staff.

You may want to use political appointees to get the programs started, but transition those programs to the careerists as soon as practicable. The later you do this in an administration, the more you risk that your successor will take your programs in a different direction.

### Maintain a sense of proportion.

The work you do will be extremely important. Unfortunately, everyone will be telling you that and how important you are as well. After a while, it may be difficult to maintain a realistic perspective. Not everything you do will be important and not every action you take will be the right one. You may even receive more criticism for doing the right thing than if you had done the wrong thing. Friends and family can be an important counterbalance to overstated compliments or unfair criticisms. Stay connected to them.

We also suggest adding "the mother test" in deciding how important things are. Imagine explaining to your mother why something is important. If you think it's unlikely she would agree, perhaps it isn't important.

### Do the job, don't be the position.

Your job carries a title, a lot of prestige, a nice office, and an attentive staff. You should concentrate on what you can accomplish from the leverage of that position. Archimedes, the ancient Greek philosopher, is purported to have said, "Give me a lever long enough and a place to stand on and I will move the world." This job gives you the lever and the place to stand.

### Don't burn your bridges.

Washington is a "society of immortals." The organization you work with today will work with you tomorrow. The people you see today you will see tomorrow, though their business cards or even their party affiliation may change. The issue you work on today will come back tomorrow in a new incarnation. Disagreements or dishonesty will be remembered. Don't burn your bridges; your ally today may be your adversary tomorrow and your ally the day after.

## Takeaways

- Manage the politics.
- Manage the stakeholder relationships, but save your personal time for the most important ones.
- Meet regularly with your senior political/career management team on agency programs.
- Don't take too long to fill important jobs or let key decisions slip.
- Empower your team, stay current with what they are doing, and focus on the big picture.
- Reward innovation, collaboration, and success.
- Manage the crises. Plan for unpleasant surprises and act quickly when they happen.
- Manage yourself. Don't let your calendar manage you.
- Find people who will tell you the truth. Listen to them.
- Embed your legacy in the career bureaucracy, not your political subordinates.
- Maintain a sense of proportion.
- Do the job, don't be the position.
- Don't burn your bridges.

# PART II: STAKEHOLDERS

# CHAPTER EIGHT

# The White House

Thurgood Marshall Jr and Christopher P. Lu

# THE WHITE HOUSE

*By Thurgood Marshall Jr and Christopher P. Lu*

In your role as a new agency leader, one of your greatest challenges will be to balance the daily demands of your job with the important task of making progress on your agency's long-term priorities and goals. One important stakeholder—if not the most important stakeholder—that can be of great assistance to you in accomplishing your agency's mission is the White House. The greater your ability to work closely and effectively with the White House, the more success your agency will enjoy. Your goal will be to have your talented team interact seamlessly with their White House counterparts, their colleagues in other executive branch agencies, and representatives in and out of government.

## Working with the White House

It is important to have realistic expectations. It is highly unlikely that you will be called to the White House on a daily basis, but you will have opportunities to interact with the White House throughout your tenure. Most of your dealings with the White House will be program- or policy–specific, or because of some crisis. When a crisis arises you will be working with White House staff intensely for a short period of time; then you will be off their radar until the next emergency situation.

Your job will be to make sure that your agency gets the most out of those interactions. You should get to know those in the White House who are assigned to or are interested in your agency. You and your staff must work to make sure that your agency is in sync with the White House.

A keen understanding of the overall White House structure, as well as which offices and staffers are in charge of various issues, will help to pave the way to a smoother working relationship when, as invariably occurs, you find yourself or members of your team presented with a project that calls for collaboration under pressure. In working with the White House, it is important to understand that it is run almost exclusively by political appointees. It works at a faster pace than departments and agencies.

While you clearly want to be responsive to the White House, you should also try to find exactly where in the White House a request is coming from. The White House is a big place with many different offices (see page 64) that are not necessarily aligned among themselves. Beware of phone calls that say, "The White House is calling." You have to find out to whom you are speaking.

It is important to understand that the White House is all about relationships. You have to develop credibility with individuals in the White House and build relationships with them. Developing trust and good relationships is important to seeking White House support for your policy initiatives and can be as important when a problem arises.

## Coordinating Your Agency Calendar and Activities with the White House

It will be incumbent upon you to build your agency calendar and activities in parallel with the administration and the White House. Political appointees must understand the White House agenda and what the White House is trying to accomplish.

With any administration, a series of action-forcing events fills its internal and external calendars. These events establish a rhythm that can help you to schedule actions and plan good news and bad news announcements. Internally, expect a blizzard of regular meetings to dictate the flow of events throughout the course of the day. Unexpected events will trigger other meetings, and your team may need to inject itself on occasion. Externally, a relentless and recurring series of events trigger activity at daily, weekly, monthly, and annual intervals. Those events can include regularly anticipated monthly reports such as economic updates, as well as breaking news.

## Working with the White House Communications Office

Your team will need to be able to interact with many of the White House offices, some more routinely than others. Your department can expect daily contact with the White House Communications Office. In many ways, communications drive everything. Messaging is important and it is important for you to engage with communications staff.

With regard to the communications operation, you will and should be expected to amplify the administration's message and its accomplishments in your meetings and speeches. By the same token, you will need to work with the White House to inject your policy initiatives and accomplishments into the message for the President, as appropriate. Internally, department staff should be in the habit of tracking the on-record and off-record exchanges that the President's press secretary has with the press corps.

Be on the lookout for constituent anecdotes that highlight the positive impact of the President's programs your agency administers so those stories can be incorporated into the presidential message process. Get a sense of the rapid response apparatus at the White House and have a plan in mind for your office to plug into that process if a crisis arises. Your department should establish a pipeline of "good news" deliverables that you can share with the President, Vice President, and their spouses. They will significantly enhance exposure for your projects and bring more breadth to the press coverage of your agency.

# At a Glance: Key White House Offices

**The Office of Cabinet Affairs** is the primary point of contact between the White House, cabinet members, and executive agency heads.

**The Office of the Chief of Staff** oversees White House staff and works with others to develop and pursue the President's agenda. This includes being the final "stop" where issues are vetted and positions taken before being presented to the President.

**The Office of Communications** is responsible for planning and producing the President's media events, and it also includes speech writing.

**The Office of Digital Strategy** is responsible for delivering the President's message to online audiences, as well as providing platforms for members of the public to connect with the administration and one another. The office develops and creates content for the White House's websites, mobile apps, email program, and official social media presences.

**The Office of the First Lady** aids the First Lady in all aspects of her public life, including the First Lady's personal initiatives.

**The Office of Legislative Affairs** serves as the President's liaison to the United States Congress.

**The Office of Presidential Personnel** recruits, screens, and recommends qualified candidates for presidential appointments to federal departments and agencies.

**The Office of Public Engagement and Intergovernmental Affairs** promotes presidential priorities through outreach to concerned constituencies and public interest groups. This includes planning White House briefings, meetings, and large events with the President, Vice President, and other White House staff. The office also serves as the President's liaison to state, local, and tribal governments.

**The Office of Scheduling and Advance** is responsible for planning, organizing, and implementing the President's daily and long-range schedules. All requests for appointments, meetings, or events with the President are directed through this office. The office coordinates all logistical arrangements for presidential visits.

**The Office of the Vice President** serves the Vice President in performing the many detailed activities pertaining to his immediate office.

**The Office of the White House Counsel** advises the President on all legal issues concerning the President and the White House.

Adapted from www.whitehouse.gov.

As a political appointee, you must also know when to flag "bad news." The White House does not like surprises. Your department needs to give people in the White House a heads-up on items that will be of interest to them. Your department may need to make a series of phone calls to different offices in the White House so nobody is surprised by the bad news. There is no central place to go in the White House, so your department will need to touch all the bases in addition to the communications office.

### Working with the White House Office of Legislative Affairs

Your congressional lobbying team ought to perform its tasks in close tandem with your counterparts throughout the executive branch and the White House. They should be attuned to the relationships that the President has with members of the House and Senate who exercise authorization or appropriation authority over your agency. That can serve as an early alert system to opportunities or potential problems on the horizon. Make sure that your department cultivates strong relationships with the House and Senate leadership on both sides of the aisle.

### Working with the White House Policy Councils

Your ability to engage with the various policy councils and strategic planning offices will be an essential component of your job, and it will require your personal time, supported by the expertise your department-wide team possesses. As you advance your agency's agenda and tackle a long list of presidential promises framed during the election campaign, keep in mind that the power of the President's pen can launch significant action. This power will be an especially welcome option during the administration's post-election transition and during periods of harsh partisanship.

While there are clearly experts in the White House with substantive expertise, you should note that they will be focused primarily on getting the policy right—not implementation. Policies can only be implemented at the department and agency levels. Implementation will be your responsibility, and it is important that you alert the White House of potential implementation challenges during the policy development process.

### Interacting with Other White House Offices

There are a number of process-oriented offices at the White House, including the Office of Cabinet Affairs and the Office of Scheduling and Advance. They will provide valuable information and opportunities. It will be important to keep those offices well-informed on events within your department.

Handled well, those individuals can act as surrogates for you within the White House operation to ferret out information and to advance your interests. When you and your team are asked to deploy in support of the President, your department should touch base with a senior member of the White House staff to make sure he or she is aware of the request so you don't find yourself working for a junior staffer rather than the President, as noted earlier.

There will also be instances when you might receive conflicting instructions from various parts of the White House. If you need to clarify conflicting instructions, your department can use the Office of Cabinet Affairs.

Important outreach offices will support your priorities and establish valuable bridges for your initiatives. The Office of Public Engagement and Intergovernmental Affairs is the foremost example. Working in tandem with those outreach efforts will yield benefits in the short term and the long term by explaining the rationale underlying your agency's programs; the collaboration also can help with promoting your agency's programs to important and influential stakeholders who can then build valuable support with key communities and interest groups.

## Don't Forget the Office of Management and Budget

Be sensitive to cues from the Office of Management and Budget (OMB). The viability of your programs will be at stake. In addition, OMB will offer a number of management cues through the President's Management Council, where you can expect that the Deputy Secretary of your department will have an important seat at the table to share your best practices and learn from others.

Every day will bring new challenges and fresh opportunities to harness your agency team's skills and expertise in ways that will enable the President to serve with great distinction. Few jobs offer such risks and rewards.

*Thurgood Marshall Jr is Partner at Morgan Lewis in Washington, D.C. He served as Assistant to the President and Cabinet Secretary in the Clinton Administration. He also served as Director of Legislative Affairs and Deputy Counsel to Vice President Al Gore. **The Honorable Christopher P. Lu** is Deputy Secretary at the Department of Labor. From 2009 to 2013, he served as Assistant to the President and Cabinet Secretary in the Obama Administration. In 2008, he served as the Executive Director of the presidential transition planning efforts.*

# CHAPTER NINE

# White House Policy Councils

Michele Jolin and Paul Weinstein, Jr.

# WHITE HOUSE POLICY COUNCILS

*By Michele Jolin and Paul Weinstein, Jr.*

Our next President has a powerful opportunity to measurably improve lives, strengthen communities, and make large-scale progress on our nation's great challenges. He or she will have ready access to the best and brightest policy minds to populate both the White House and the cabinet and as a source of the latest and best research and ideas. The President's policy councils—the Domestic Policy Council (DPC), National Security Council (NSC), National Economic Council (NEC), and the various statutory policy offices such as the Council of Economic Advisers (CEA)—will play a central role in designing and advocating for the policy approaches that will shape the President's success and legacy.

On a daily basis, the President, his or her cabinet, and their policy teams will make choices about, for example, how to remove obstacles to social mobility and harness the best available information to make sure that limited resources are used wisely. Political appointees need to work seamlessly with the policy councils on any issues that are—or could be—a priority to the President, in order to ensure alignment and successful implementation. Political appointees who develop a good working relationship with the policy councils are likely to have more influence in the White House than those appointees who do not spend as much time with the councils. In addition, working closely with the policy councils will assist appointees with enlisting White House support in the implementation of their programs, which impact the lives of millions of Americans.

While members of the President's cabinet are critical to policy making and execution, policy councils have the advantage of proximity—they are, more often than not, steps away from the Oval Office, and policy council staff often have close relationships with other White House officials involved in shaping the President's agenda. Policy council staff may play a gatekeeper role for important policy documents such as the State of the Union or the President's Budget, or the priority of a particular announcement. A close relationship with the policy council staff, and having an understanding their roles, will help you further improve the impact of the President's policy agenda.

## Understanding Policy Councils

Maintaining a strong and communicative relationship with the following relevant White House Policy Councils is a key to achieving progress on your agency's major policy initiatives:

- **National Security Council (NSC).** Established in 1947, the National Security Council is "the President's principal forum" for national security and foreign policy. Similar to the domestic councils, the NSC advises the President on national security and foreign policy and helps coordinate the work of the related cabinet agencies.

Members of the NSC include the Vice President, Secretary of Defense, and Secretary of State.

In 2009, President Obama approved a Presidential Study Directive-1 recommendation to merge the NSC staff and the Homeland Security Council (HSC) staff into one national security staff under the National Security Advisor. The NSC is now the President's principal forum for considering homeland security matters that require presidential determination. In addition, the NSC now also contains a cybersecurity office, headed by the U.S. Cybersecurity Coordinator, which works closely with the Federal Chief Information Officer, the Federal Chief Technology Officer, and the National Economic Council. The office was created as a result of the administration's 2009 Cyberspace Policy Review.

Over the years, the power and size of the NSC have fluctuated, and during the Bush Administration and President Obama's first term, the Council grew considerably in size. In the last two years, however, there has been a concerted effort to reduce the size of the NSC.

Originally designed to focus on policy development and coordination, the NSC over time became increasingly involved in policy implementation, reaching its zenith during the Nixon Administration. However, in recent years it has refocused more of its efforts on policy development.

- **Domestic Policy Council (DPC).** The White House has had a domestic policy staff since at least the 1960s, but the Domestic Policy Council, as we know it today, was established in 1993 by President Bill Clinton when he split the Office of Policy Development into the DPC and the National Economic Council (NEC). The President chairs the DPC, and members include the Vice President and the domestically-focused cabinet secretaries. It focuses on the President's domestic policy agenda—which includes everything from education to immigration, climate change, health policy, justice, and civil rights, to name a few.

- **National Economic Council (NEC).** The NEC advises the President on U.S. and global economic policy. Like the DPC, the NEC has a director who works in conjunction with heads of cabinet agencies.

The NEC operation is very closely modeled on the NSC. An assistant to the President leads the office with two or more deputies (one who typically focuses on domestic economic policy and the other who focuses on international economic matters), and it is staffed with political appointees who are experts in a range of areas from health care to tax policy. Like the NSC, the NEC has regular meetings with its agency members. Although it has a much smaller staff, the NEC has a much greater number of member agencies than the NSC. Recently, the Council has begun to co-author publicly released papers on policy issues with other White House offices.

## Roles Played by the White House Policy Councils

The various policy councils are typically staffed by very accomplished policy experts and leaders. Those working with them should understand the environment in which they operate, as well as the role they play in the White House. Policy councils serve as, among other things:

- Gatekeepers for the President's policy priorities, and at times, the President
- An in-house think tank—generating and vetting ideas
- Executors of the President's ideas and delegators of both information and responsibilities
- More often than not, the final word on policy disputes

The policy councils are very different from other units in the Executive Office of the President or cabinet-level departments. First, they have no programmatic and regulatory responsibilities or specific constituencies beyond the President. This lack of programmatic or regulatory bias can help increase the perceived legitimacy of their role in the policy-making process but can be easily lost if they do not act as "honest brokers" in handling agency disputes.

Second, the staffs of the policy councils are primarily made up of political appointments not subject to Senate confirmation. As such, policy council staffs have the ability to impact the decision-making process during the first days of a new administration. However, while the councils are more flexible, they can also lack the agencies' expertise, and turnover is relatively high, which creates a lack of continuity on policy matters. The lack of expertise provides an opportunity for agencies to influence the councils by providing policy experts in a number of fields to work with the councils.

Finally, each President puts his or her own stamp on the process for making policy and which voices have the most influence, but one constant remains: the increasing complexity of the President's job and the speed at which the administration must work to succeed. The fact that policy councils are typically small groups comprised of close aides to the President, and that their staffs tend to have strong relationships throughout the White House complex, contributes to their significant influence. Unlike the cabinet agencies, the policy councils tend to operate largely out of the public eye, with the exception of the heads of each council often having some public-facing or spokesperson role.

## Collaboration, Coordination, and Communication with the White House Policy Councils

Succeeding within the, at times, dizzying inner workings of the executive branch of the federal government requires skillful collaboration, constant coordination, and effective communication, as well as an awareness of the role communication plays in policy deployment.

# Executive Office of the President Statutory Offices

In addition to the three White House Councils discussed in this chapter, there are also several important statutory offices within the Executive Office of the President (EOP) with whom agency political executives will also interact. Unlike the White House Councils, the heads of these statutory offices must be Senate confirmed and are asked to testify before Congress on matters of policy. They can also have programmatic, regulatory, or reporting responsibilities. Key statutory offices include:

**The Council of Economic Advisers (CEA)** is charged with offering the President objective economic advice on formulating both domestic and international economic policy. The Council bases its recommendations and analysis on economic research and empirical evidence, using the best data available to support the President in setting our nation's economic policy. CEA was established by the Employment Act of 1946.

**The Council on Environmental Quality (CEQ**) coordinates federal environmental efforts and works closely with agencies and other White House offices in developing environmental policies and initiatives. CEQ was established by the National Environmental Policy Act of 1969 (NEPA), with additional responsibilities provided by the Environmental Quality Improvement Act of 1970.

**The Office of National Drug Control Policy (ONDCP)** advises the President on drug-control issues, coordinates drug-control activities and related funding across the federal government, and produces the annual National Drug Control Strategy, which outlines administration efforts to reduce illicit drug use, manufacturing and trafficking, drug-related crime and violence, and drug-related health consequences. ONDCP was established by the Anti-Drug Abuse Act of 1988.

**The Office of Science and Technology Policy (OSTP)** provides the President and his senior staff with accurate, relevant, and timely scientific and technical advice on all matters of consequence; ensures that the executive branch policies are informed by sound science; and ensures that the scientific and technical executive branch work is properly coordinated so as to provide the greatest benefit to society. OSTP was established by the National Science and Technology Policy, Organization, and Priorities Act of 1976.

**The Office of the U.S. Trade Representative (USTR)** is responsible for developing and coordinating U.S. international trade, commodity, and direct investment policy and overseeing negotiations with other countries. USTR was established as part of the Trade Expansion Act of 1962, with additional responsibilities assigned by the Trade Act of 1974.

Adapted from www.whitehouse.gov/administration/eop

- **Collaboration.** To be effective in creating or advocating for policy priorities, you should find ways to collaborate with the White House Policy
  Councils as well as other political appointees, career civil servants across
  the agencies, and members of Congress and their staff. This collaboration makes for better policy design, but as importantly, it will increase the
  likelihood of successful execution and implementation.
- **Coordination.** This work also requires coordination to address the host
  of cross-cutting policy issues (e.g. education, energy, trade, job creation,
  etc.) and to make sure that policies complement one another. As the
  President's time is a precious resource and his or her stay in the White
  House is relatively short, there will also be a natural tension over which
  policy priorities should take precedence. Policy staff at agencies must
  work together with their colleagues on the policy councils—including
  allowing for a complete airing of all sides of an issue when needed—so
  the President has the best possible information with which to make a
  decision.
- **Communication.** In order to be an effective advocate for their agencies
  or issue areas, policymakers at all levels must effectively communicate
  their policy priorities and how those policies will improve the lives of the
  American people. Success will also, at times, necessitate frequent collaboration with the White House communications team to ensure that
  policy priorities are well-timed and relevant to the President's message
  and to advancing the administration's agenda. In the media-driven world
  of politics, and increasingly policy, a compelling case for policy priorities
  and a strong relationship with the White House communications team will
  help policymakers get their ideas in front of the people who will decide
  what the President and the entire administration talk about on a daily,
  weekly, and monthly basis. After all, every communications product from
  the State of the Union Address to the White House daily press briefing
  requires a foundation rooted in good policy.

## Conclusion

The policy councils can make the difference between your success and
failure, and you need to develop a good and effective working relationship
with them. While you both report to the President, as a practical matter the
policy councils have a more direct relationship with the President on a day-
to-day basis. If you want to include a proposal in the President's State of the
Union address, you will need the sign-off of one of the policy councils. If you
want to appeal a budget decision by OMB, you will need a policy council on
your side. If you are caught in a policy dispute with another agency, you will
need the assistance of a policy council to arbitrate the disagreement.

**Michele Jolin** is the Chief Executive Officer and co-founder of Results for America. She served as Chief of Staff for the Council of Economic Advisers under President Bill Clinton and as a Senior Advisor for Social Innovation for the Domestic Policy Council under President Barack Obama. **Paul Weinstein, Jr.** directs the Masters Program in Public Management at the Johns Hopkins University. He served as Special Assistant to the President and Chief of Staff of the Domestic Policy Council during the Clinton Administration. He also served as Senior Advisor for Policy Planning and Coordination to Vice President Al Gore.

# CHAPTER TEN

# Office of Management and Budget

Kathy Stack

# OFFICE OF MANAGEMENT AND BUDGET

*By Kathy Stack*

The Office of Management and Budget (OMB) is sometimes described as "the most powerful organization in government that no one's ever heard of." In your new position, you will interact with its staff on a regular basis. Every major issue involving budget resources, legislation, regulations, or government-wide management priorities passes through OMB.

To help achieve your objectives, you should build strong relationships with OMB's political appointees and staff and encourage your managers to do the same. Your primary contact will be your Program Associate Director (PAD) who oversees your agency's budget and program issues, as well as those of related agencies. You should also build ties with career staff who have direct influence over your agency's activities. These include the Deputy Associate Director (DAD) and the Branch Chief who handle your agency (both career Senior Executive Service members), as well as program examiners who analyze your programs. In addition, engage key staff in OMB's regulatory and management offices who will be reviewing your agency's proposals.

You may find it unnerving, at first, to engage directly with OMB's career civil servants rather than political appointees. Get over it. These dedicated career staff will be providing analyses and recommendations to OMB leadership and the President's senior advisors on a regular basis. If you want them advocating on your behalf, work closely with them.

## How OMB Serves the President

During every administration, the President and White House senior advisors come to rely on OMB for its institutional expertise on how to get things done through administrative action when feasible and appropriate, and through congressional legislation when necessary. OMB helps the President in key ways:

- **OMB asks probing questions to assess whether an agency's existing programs, and its proposed initiatives, fit with administration priorities and if the agency can manage them effectively.** These questions include:
  - Are the policy objectives compelling and consistent with the President's priorities?
  - Do credible data and evidence demonstrate that programs or proposed initiatives will achieve their objectives?
  - Is there strong coordination with other government or private sector activities that support related objectives?
  - Does the agency have the capacity to manage its programs well, measure their impact, and continuously improve?

- **OMB aligns resources with the President's priorities.** In every annual budget cycle, OMB helps the President reassess how federal resources should be allocated to further the President's priorities. With its comprehensive knowledge of all government agencies and programs, OMB advises the President on what investments are likely to have the greatest impact, and on what programs and activities are not achieving important objectives and should be candidates for reform, reduction, or elimination.
- **OMB coordinates policies and implementation strategies across agencies.** OMB works with White House policy councils to coordinate development and implementation of cross-cutting programmatic policies such as immigration, climate change, and poverty reduction. It shares best practices to help agencies build capacity to use data and evidence to improve decision making.

    OMB also develops the President's "Management Agenda" to tackle government-wide management challenges in areas such as IT acquisition, contracting, financial management, and personnel. The Deputy Director for Management at OMB chairs the President's Management Council, comprised primarily of Deputy Secretaries from major agencies and the heads of the Office of Personnel Management (OPM) and the General Services Administration (GSA). When disasters or emergencies require quick, coordinated action by multiple agencies, OMB often orchestrates the administration's response.
- **OMB helps eliminate barriers to policy implementation.** When current laws, regulations, or administrative processes impede government's capacity to accomplish agency missions, OMB identifies options for overcoming those barriers. Often, the barriers are administrative, and they can be removed through waivers or common sense reinterpretations of outdated policy guidance issued by OMB or agencies. When barriers are regulatory, OMB works with agencies to modify regulations. When impediments are statutory, OMB helps determine the most effective, practical strategy for securing legislative change.
- **OMB reviews regulations and how agencies collect and use information.** OMB's Office of Information and Regulatory Affairs (OIRA) plays a key role in how your agency issues regulations, as well as how it collects and uses information. By statute, OIRA must approve any effort your agency takes to collect information from 10 or more people, as well as any policy that requires 10 or more people to retain or disclose information. Under an Executive Order that has been renewed by each President since 1980, OIRA reviews all significant proposed and final regulations before they can be released to the public. Agencies rely heavily on both of these processes—collecting information and regulations—to implement their policies and programs. As a result, understanding the processes and criteria that OIRA uses to make decisions will give you a significant advantage in achieving your goals, as will getting to know the OIRA leadership and staff who coordinate with other parts of OMB, other White House offices,

# What About "Management?"
*By Jonathan D. Breul*

The "m" for "management" in OMB was inserted into the name of the reorganized Bureau of the Budget in 1970 to give prominence to the notion that the central budget agency in the executive branch should give as much time to improving the quality of management as it does to preparing the budget and developing presidential policy. Neither good policies nor good investments are likely to work, let alone succeed, if they are undermined by poor implementation. For this reason, OMB plays a key role overseeing agency management of programs and resources to achieve legislative goals and administration policy.

There are four key offices within the management side of OMB, each of which is headed by a political appointee and reports to the Deputy Director for Management:

- **Office of Federal Financial Management (OFFM)** develops government-wide policies and provides strategic direction to improve financial management, reporting, and systems; to reduce improper payments; to improve grants management; and to "right-size" federal real property. OFFM also coordinates the activities of agency chief financial officers and senior real property officers.

- **Office of Federal Procurement Policy (OFPP)** is responsible for setting government-wide acquisition priorities and policies, which shape the full range of federal agency procurement practices. In addition to its formal role in developing procurement regulations for the entire federal government, OFPP works with agencies to strengthen the acquisition workforce, and it initiates and fosters cost-saving and risk-reduction practices across the government. OFPP also works to ensure that agencies rely on and manage contractors in fiscally responsible ways.

- **Office of E-Government and Information Technology (E-Gov),** headed by the federal government chief information officer, develops and provides direction in the use of Internet-based technologies to make it easier for citizens and businesses to interact with the federal government, save taxpayer dollars, and streamline citizen participation. E-Gov houses the U.S. Digital Service, which is comprised of teams of problem solvers helping agencies simplify their technology services for citizens, making services more efficient and effective.

- **Office of Performance and Personnel Management (OPPM)** leads the effort to drive mission-focused performance gains across the federal government. OPPM coordinates the administration's goal-setting and performance review process for agencies' high-priority performance goals and guides agencies' strategic and annual planning, performance reviews, and performance reporting. OPPM also functions as the Resource Management Office for the Office of Personnel Management (OPM) and guides federal personnel policy, working closely with OPM to implement effective personnel policies and practices.

Agency leaders and managers must work with OMB on a wide range of management issues. While your basic or *primary* point of contact remains the program examiner in the Resource Management Office, smart agency leaders and managers work closely with OMB to develop a well-thought-out management strategy. Creating such a strategy may require agency heads to work with several OMB offices, each with their own perspectives. With effort and the creation of an effective working relationship, agency officials can work toward making these relationships a shared approach to achieving the results the administration, Congress, and the public expect.

*Jonathan D. Breul is an Adjunct Professor at Georgetown University's Graduate Public Policy Institute. He was formerly the Executive Director of the IBM Center for The Business of Government. During his government career, he served as the Senior Advisor to the Deputy Director of Management in the Office of Management and Budget.*

and other interested agencies to oversee your agency's regulatory and information policy.

## How to Harness OMB's Expertise to Further Your Agency's Objectives

OMB's government-wide perspective, policy expertise, and knowledge of all the levels of government are assets that agency leaders can tap to advance important policy and operational objectives. Here are tips for doing so:

- **From the outset, build strong relationships with both political and career staff at OMB.** Get to know your OMB Program Associate Director (PAD), who regularly meets with the OMB Director and White House Policy Councils and often negotiates with congressional committees on authorization and appropriations bills. Because your PAD's time is limited, foster close ties with the DAD, Branch Chief, and examiners that oversee your key programs. If you have regulatory and management priorities, reach out to OMB political appointees and career staff in those offices too.

  An early "get acquainted" session with OMB staff can pay dividends throughout your tenure. Invite the PAD, DAD, and Branch Chief overseeing your agency to meet with you. Also involve OMB program examiners and regulatory or management analysts that work on important initiatives tied to your priorities. If you understand each other's perspectives and agree on common goals, your future interactions will be more productive and your proposals will get more serious consideration.

- **Engage OMB early on important proposals.** Every agency must abide by OMB's formal deadlines for submitting budgets, which often include related legislative proposals. Agencies launch their internal budget development process each spring and transmit their final budget recommendations to OMB in mid-September. Agencies that don't preview their major proposals with OMB before September often resent OMB's criticism of proposals they spent months developing. This can be avoided by discussing preliminary proposals in the spring or early summer so OMB can identify the hard questions the agency will need to address, share tips and best practices that could strengthen proposals, and facilitate connections with other parts of government working on related issues. With a strong September submission, you and OMB can focus on developing a robust implementation strategy in the fall that is coordinated with other government efforts and more likely to gain traction in Congress.

- **Acknowledge any problems related to your agency's capacity to perform its mission and seek OMB's advice to address them.** In every administration, new political appointees are surprised by gaps in agency expertise and bureaucratic processes that stymie their ability to effectively accomplish their agency's mission. One common reaction is to seek funding for additional staff, which leads to frustration and inaction when OMB or Congress rejects the request because of funding constraints. A better strategy is to seek OMB's advice on how to tackle your agency's administrative challenges. OMB may be able to identify expertise in your own agency or elsewhere in government you were not aware of, suggest ways to leverage non-governmental expertise, or debunk myths preventing your agency from adopting more efficient, innovative practices.

- **Avoid communication breakdowns.** It's common for agency-OMB relations to become adversarial when OMB rejects agency proposals or exposes management deficiencies. Some agency leaders react by going around OMB (to Congress or other White House offices) or limiting staff interactions with OMB. This is self-defeating. Your best chance of achieving your goals is to obtain OMB support for your vision, have candid discussions about how to achieve it, and empower your staff to work with OMB on implementation. By building a partnership, you will have opportunities to offer OMB constructive feedback on how its activities are helping or hindering your agency's progress (e.g., when OMB's internal operations are uncoordinated). Importantly, when OMB career employees help an agency implement successful reforms, they will be powerful advocates for sustaining those achievements after you leave office.

In sum, treat OMB as an action enabler rather than an obstacle. That partnership can help you and your staff make big things happen.

*Kathy Stack is Vice President of Evidence-Based Innovation at the Laura and John Arnold Foundation. She served 27 years at the Office of Management and Budget.*

# CHAPTER ELEVEN

# Congress

Richard B. Beutel

# CONGRESS

*By Richard B. Beutel*

The genius of the American political system lies in its separation of powers—the core constitutional principle of checks and balances regulating the governance of the American people. Appointees in a new administration will naturally initially be focused upon the many operational challenges confronting their agencies. However, new officials must nonetheless be sensitive to the role of Congress in the American system of government. Managing the agency's relationship with Congress requires thought, care, and patience.

The inevitable tension between Congress and the executive branch often creates inter-branch conflict. It is imperative to manage this tension. It is best to think of Congress as a difficult in-law—one whose goodwill and cooperation is essential to a happy marriage. Successfully navigating this relationship is essential to the agency's mission success.

The power of Congress over an executive branch agency stems from three discrete responsibilities rooted in the Constitution:

- **Authorization:** Congress creates agencies and revises programs through the authorization and reauthorization process.
- **Appropriations:** Congress enacts the budgets necessary for agencies to operate through the appropriations process.
- **Oversight:** Congress monitors how agencies spend taxpayer money through its oversight process.

Each of these responsibilities must be accommodated under our system of government because only Congress has the authority to appropriate budget dollars to federal agencies, and Congress plays a key role in overseeing the agencies in terms of day-to-day operational effectiveness.

It is these multiple roles—authorization, appropriations, and oversight—that create the imperative that senior agency executives develop and maintain an effective relationship with Congress.

## What Motivates Congress?

In approaching Congress, it is helpful to know what motivates individual members of Congress. They appear to be primarily driven by a combination of constituent concerns and reelection. Remember that representatives in the House are reelected every two years, while reelections occur every six years in the Senate. House members, accordingly, are in constant reelection mode because of their election cycle short tenure. As a result, House hearings often tend to be politically charged, superficial, and headline-focused. In terms of the agencies, most "gotcha" style hearings happen in the House.

The Senate is very different from the House. The Senate plays the role of the deliberative body, and it is intended to be a counterweight to the populist currents that flow through the House. As a result, Senate hearings usually tend to be more deliberative, substantive, and in-depth.

## The Importance of Fostering Openness and Transparency with Congress

Nothing will draw unwelcome congressional attention faster than appearing to stonewall legitimate congressional inquiries. Therefore, it is common sense to develop open and transparent communications with Congress. Senior agency officials must ensure that agency staff are honest, transparent, and responsive to congressional inquiries.

Each agency has an Office of Legislative Affairs. This office is responsible for day-to-day interactions with Congress. The office is an essential stakeholder in the agency's relationship with Congress. Over time, however, legislative staff may begin to view their jobs in adversarial terms with Congress. This can lead to staffers obstructing or hampering legitimate congressional inquiries. Agency executives must ensure that their legislative office understands that the job is to facilitate transparent, open communications and not to appear to obstruct congressional oversight, however unfair that perception may be for the legislative affairs staff.

Agency executives are responsible for ensuring that congressional inquiries are answered in a full and timely fashion. While congressional inquiries can become onerous and expensive, timely and complete responses are essential to preserve the trusting relationship. Don't resort to cheap tricks, such as dumping heavily redacted documents on congressional staffers on a Friday at 5 p.m. or before a major holiday. Don't redact documents in an unjustifiable fashion. Provide the responses fully, completely, on time, and in digital form, if at all possible.

If the response to a congressional inquiry is delayed, agency leadership should take the lead to proactively explain why the delay has occurred and offer a credible timeframe for a full response. If critical information is omitted, explain why it is omitted in a complete and transparent fashion.

Agency officials should note that the courts interpret attempts to withhold agency documents and information on the grounds of attorney-client privilege and executive deliberative privilege in a very stringent fashion. Congress also views them as attempts to stonewall or obstruct congressional oversight. Take care when relying upon such arguments as the basis to withhold information from Congress.

## Interacting with Authorizing Committees

Most congressional committees are authorizing committees. These committees have jurisdiction over the legislation that created your agency and its programs. These committees typically have more in-depth understanding of how your agency works and have a longer-term view of issues.

Many programs are authorized for a time-limited period as a way of ensuring a look back at how programs are managed and how effective they are. When you begin work at your agency, find out the timeframes for various programs' reauthorizations; oftentimes these will frame your action timetable. See if your agency has program evaluations underway on the effectiveness of existing programs; these can be useful foundations for reauthorizing programs or reframing them in order to be more effective in the future.

Authorizing committees also conduct oversight hearings on the ongoing operations of programs, not just when they are scheduled to be reauthorized.

## Interacting with Appropriations Committees

The congressional appropriations process creates many challenges for the executive branch agencies. Along with oversight responsibilities, Congress also holds the "power of the purse strings" for each federal agency. This constitutionally-mandated prerogative is closely guarded by the various appropriations subcommittees that have jurisdiction over your agency's programs. Therefore, a smart agency executive will take pains to develop individual relationships with the appropriations committee congressmen (and their staffers) that govern the agency budget. Don't wait for a budget crisis or funding challenge to cultivate these relationships. It is essential to establish an open and transparent line of communication with agency appropriators.

In addition, keep in mind that the worst thing an agency executive can allow is for the appropriators to be surprised or blindsided by bad news. It is always better to meet proactively, in regular dialogue, and to carefully honor a relationship of trust and transparency with congressional appropriators. Only in this fashion can agencies ensure that they receive the necessary resources to successfully achieve their missions.

## Interacting with Oversight Committees

Ensuring that your congressional communications are transparent, credible, and complete in response to congressional inquiries does not end with the congressional oversight committees. Other oversight stakeholders, such as GAO, act as the research arm of the legislative branch. GAO should also be extended full and transparent cooperation by agency officials, as cooperation with its staff is essential for open and transparent congressional relationships.

When it comes to congressional oversight, agencies should not regard Congress as an adversary. Constitutionally, Congress and the executive branch have a joint responsibility to deliver services to the American people. When Congress comes calling, they are just doing their jobs.

## Other Congressional Dynamics

Congress is not a unified entity any more than the executive branch or an administration. You need to be sensitive to such dynamics in order to be effective. For example:

- **There are well-known differences between Democrats and Republicans.** Sometimes, however, the two sides will join forces on issues when there are House vs. Senate prerogatives at stake, or when committee jurisdiction over an issue, program, or agency is in contention. These are not uncommon.
- **Agencies often have to deal with different committees on various issues.** Issues that fall into the bounds of authorization, appropriation, and oversight committees are more common. But for many agencies, there are oftentimes multiple authorization committees and several different appropriation subcommittees involved. Some agencies have a large number of committees with jurisdiction over the agency or programs. For example, 77 different committees or subcommittees reportedly oversee the Environmental Protection Agency, and the Department of Homeland Security reports to 108 committees and subcommittees. The committees have different agendas and priorities and they typically do not coordinate with each other, leaving your agency to navigate issues.
- **There are also differences between committee staffs and the staffs of individual members of Congress.** Oftentimes, the committee staffs have more subject matter expertise. Generally, members' staffs are calling about individual constituent issues. Knowing the differences in who is calling can help prioritize and frame any responses.

In general, as noted earlier, your legislative affairs office can help you navigate the eccentricities of the congressional process.

Finally, if not properly handled, congressional relations can greatly hamper the effective operation of a federal agency. Poor communications, distrust, and acrimony with members of Congress and their staff can result in lost funding, onerous and lengthy oversight, and the agency's failure to achieve its goals and aspirations. Agency and congressional relationships are an area fraught with challenges that must be carefully managed.

*Richard A. Beutel is Principal at Cyrrus Analytics LLC. He previously served as a Senior Advisor to the House Committee on Oversight and Government Reform and as Senior Counsel to the Senate Committee on Homeland Security and Government Affairs.*

## CHAPTER TWELVE

# Cross-Agency Collaborators

Jane E. Fountain

# CROSS-AGENCY COLLABORATORS

*By Jane E. Fountain*

One of political appointees' newer tasks in the next administration will be to continue to move the federal government toward more effective cross-agency collaboration. The Government Performance and Results Modernization Act (GPRAMA) of 2010 requires collaboration across agencies, from consultation and knowledge sharing to joint policy making and operations. Political appointees now need to increase their understanding of how to effectively implement cross-agency collaboration.

GPRAMA's passage recognizes contemporary political realities. First, complex policy problems, such as export promotion, disaster preparedness, and food safety, cannot be addressed by a single agency. Second, economic constraints make it increasingly problematic to continue spending on redundant and overlapping programs, services, and systems. Third, collaboration across agencies allows the federal government to streamline, simplify, and improve policy making and implementation. Collaboration has the potential to:
- Save money
- Simplify government for citizens and business
- Make public managers more productive

According to Donald Kettl, University of Maryland, "interwoven governance" has evolved over time, with lines blurring between programs, agencies, levels of government, and even public-private sectors. This blurring occurs in healthcare, environmental areas, and human services. Collaboration is a key strategy for coping with this blurring, starting back in the Clinton Administration. For example, the 1999 cross-agency e-commerce working group reviewed laws, regulations, technical standards, and licensing requirements that impeded e-commerce and recommended changes. In the George W. Bush Administration, the Quicksilver Initiatives in 2001 focused on making cross-agency electronic networks central to the delivery of services to the public, rather than the traditional agency-centric approach. The Obama Administration took this a step further, creating "cross-agency priority goals" that reach across agency boundaries.

Why is this trend toward greater collaboration important? A recent report on the root causes behind why agencies wind up on GAO's list of programs at the highest risk for failure is because they were ineffective in managing cross-boundary issues related to program implementation.

This chapter's basic message is this: Cross-agency collaboration is sustainable if, and only if, executives operate strategically within their institutional environments and develop two types of cross-agency collaboration:
- **Collaboration through people:** Relationship skills must be developed for effective executives and teams. Team-building skills are those used by

executives willing and able to work across jurisdictional boundaries to develop effective professional relationships and cohesive working groups. Effective executives need skills including active listening, fairness, and respect—qualities that produce trust in a cross-agency collaborative initiative. In cross-boundary teams, executives build informal relationships outside regular hierarchical channels. Teams function well when productive communities based on trust and professional experience form around a problem, project, or practice.

- **Collaboration through processes:** In addition to effective executives and effective teams, cross-agency collaborative initiatives need effective organizational processes, which include a focus on strategy, operations, systems, and their management. Effective organizational processes demand an organizational skill set that emphasizes rigor and clarity in setting goals, designing systems, building in milestones, attracting resources, and framing an organization that lies across agency boundaries.

To accomplish cross-agency collaboration, appointees need to use both relationship skills and organizational structures strategically, working within institutional constraints. The lessons reported in this chapter bring together a wide range of practical research, more than two decades of studying cross-boundary relationships, and working with government managers in the U.S. and other countries. This article provides a comprehensive approach to cross-agency collaboration. It is not enough for an executive to develop the interpersonal skills of persuasion or negotiation. Nor is it enough for a manager to focus exclusively on organizational processes such as performance and measurement.

Appointees who concentrate exclusively on passing new laws and budgets will miss other key dimensions of cross-agency collaboration. Management advice and research abound on collaborative governance, networked governance, joined-up governance, and more. Some advice emphasizes individual leadership skills in developing collaboration. Other studies emphasize building networks for innovation. Still others focus on social media and technologies that should somehow make self-organization possible. And others stress performance management with an emphasis on clear goals, measures, and accountability. Cross-agency collaboration demands all of these skills and more.

## Implementing Cross-Agency Initiatives

What do appointees do to build a major cross-agency effort? The actions below are essentials.

**Set and communicate clear, compelling direction and goals.** Build commitment to a cross-agency vision, mission, long- and near-term goals, and objectives. Frame the effort, set the direction, and establish the culture as one

# Key Ingredients for Successfully Implementing a Cross-Agency Initiative

- **Relationship skills.** Build and use relationship skills to be effective across agency boundaries. Be prepared to use persuasion, influence, and negotiation. Executives engender trust and commitment by delivering on promises and treating collaborating members with respect. Employ active listening, empathy, and respect to be sure that all relevant partners are heard and their particular constraints are acknowledged and understood. Invest the time required to build strong professional relationships.

- **Teams.** Build teams that work. Develop and sustain shared commitment among a core group of managers who will be central to the effort. A cross-agency program consists of executive, management, and several working group teams. Working groups will model their behavior on the tone set by core executive and management teams.

  As part of building teams, executives must resolve or buffer conflicts so that the collaboration can do its work. Sometimes, officials at an executive level must act to resolve conflict or change leadership or structure. Replace those who will not commit to the collaboration and its strategy.

- **Professional networks.** Leverage existing professional networks where they exist rather than trying to build a network from scratch. They are found in every functional area of management: finance, budget, IT, loans, grants management, procurement, etc., and in many policy domains. Members of these networks tend to know who the natural leaders are and know reputations based on past performance.

- **Shared learning.** Adapt the work and scope of teams and networks through real-time shared learning. Continue to incorporate perspectives and feedback but manage (or deny) requests for change that would be costly or shift direction. Adapt to changes in the environment. Cross-agency collaborations must continue to improve, refine, and adapt to changing technologies, legislation, stakeholder needs, and other environmental dimensions, so keep cross-agency management and executive groups intact and meeting intermittently.

that requires collaboration. Convince key managers that the new collaboration will produce better results than the status quo. An important overarching goal, a vision of the future, is a strong motivator and provides the initial logic for organizing the initiative. Keep the overarching goal and its benefits at the forefront through communication and framing.

**Fit the working group structure to the task.** Collaborative initiatives require different types of authority structures and division of labor, depending upon scale, scope, urgency, and core task dimensions. Decide on an appropriate structure and define exactly what that will mean in terms of authority, resources, and division of labor. For example, some cross-agency collaborations are organized with a lead agency that supplies services to other agencies on a fee-for-service basis. GPRAMA requires creating a set of cross-agency priority (CAP) goals. These are typically led by a White House official, but the organizational structure of the cross-agency relationships is left undetermined. The lead agency or managing partner approach differs across projects with respect to how much joint decision making and problem solving will be used.

**Establish specific roles and responsibilities.** Who will do what? Who is responsible for what? Develop clear decision-making processes including conflict resolution measures. Cross-agency collaborations require strong executive and management groups and well-organized working groups.

**Develop formal agreements.** Codify in writing what is to be accomplished, and the principal means and the timeline for accomplishment. Formalize the collaborative arrangement. Revisit this document frequently. Making formal agreements public provides accountability and transparency. It exerts pressure on cross-agency members to fulfill commitments. As part of the formal agreement, create a work plan working backward from major goals to establish interim goals and milestones. Establish and enforce clear deadlines.

**Develop shared operations and shared resources that support achieving the goal.** These range from producing shared brochures and web pages to developing shared systems and standards; co-location, shared services, and information; fee-for-service operations; standardizing and streamlining to produce consistent operations across agencies; and consolidation. For joint policy-making efforts, coordination across agencies that share responsibility for key policy challenges—such as the CAP goals—may mean communication and joint planning to align strategies that are then implemented in parallel.

Many cross-agency projects have had to generate their own resources through sharing, borrowing, or otherwise leveraging existing resources. Similarly, many have been staffed with those on short-term details from several agencies. Many executives are excellent at bootstrapping until more consistent resources become available. Moreover, cross-agency collaborations must explicitly develop and include key internal stakeholders and external stakeholders (clients and constituents) to mobilize support.

**Build shared performance metrics.** During the Obama Administration, the Department of Veterans Affairs and Department of Housing and Urban Development set a joint goal to eliminate chronic homelessness among veterans. A key element of that initiative was developing a common metric of what constitutes "chronic homelessness" so they could gauge progress. Until this was done, the two departments had not been able to coordinate efforts effectively and hold each other jointly accountable. These metrics may provide an impetus for other efforts. Performance measures are necessary to enable tracking, monitoring, and measurement/evaluation of output and outcomes across agencies and programs. Measurement is important, but without consequences, measurements lack force. Align incentives, rewards, and sanctions.

**Jane E. Fountain** is Distinguished University Professor in Political Science and Public Policy and Adjunct Professor of Computer Science at the University of Massachusetts Amherst. She is the founder and Director of the National Center for Digital Government and the Science, Technology and Society Initiative, based at the University of Massachusetts Amherst.

# CHAPTER THIRTEEN

# Interagency Councils

Steve Brockelman and Dave Mader

# INTERAGENCY COUNCILS

*By Steve Brockelman and Dave Mader*

While it's common to think of the U.S. federal government as a single massive organization, the reality is that it operates more as a federation of many distinct departments and agencies. These organizations have their own missions, budgets, governance structures, and operating cultures. Left to their own devices, agencies tend to pursue their objectives independently. But when agencies are called upon to solve challenges that cut across agencies—which is happening more and more frequently—they must learn to work together effectively.

Nowhere is this more evident than in providing the support services vital for effective mission delivery—contracting, finance, human capital, IT, and performance management. These so-called "mission-support services" are actually quite similar from agency to agency. The job of a Chief Information Officer (CIO) job in the Department of Agriculture, for example, is not so different from that of a CIO in the Department of Housing and Urban Development. Because of this, federal government officials frequently work across agencies to collaboratively tackle shared challenges and develop mission-support policies.

Perhaps the best mechanism for cross-agency collaboration among mission-support functions is the group of federal interagency management councils, collectively known as the "CXO Councils." These are long-standing councils of agency officials, most of which are established by law, who lead mission-support functions within the 24 largest federal agencies. Each CXO Council is chaired by the senior-most official at the corresponding management office in the Office of Management and Budget (OMB), with a leading career agency CXO often serving as Vice Chair.

The CXO Councils work along two dimensions:
- **Horizontally:** Peers come together from across government to identify common "pain points," to share what's working (and what isn't), and to gain a broader perspective on their evolving roles in supporting their agencies.
- **Vertically:** Councils serve as a forum to connect OMB with agency CXOs to discuss policy priorities and management plans. In response, agencies have the opportunity to collectively voice concerns about draft proposals and recommend approaches that will improve policy implementation and outcomes.

If you are a mission support leader in your department or agency, you will find yourself wearing two hats that parallel the councils' dimensions. Horizontally, you will find yourself working with other mission support colleagues in your agency (chief information officers, chief human capital officers, chief

acquisition officers, chief financial officers, and performance improvement officers). Likewise, vertically, you will have three interrelated roles:
- Ensuring compliance with government-wide requirements imposed by law, OMB, OPM, or GSA
- Ensuring the delivery of services to your customers
- Serving as an advisor to agency leaders on issues for which you are the expert

The most well-known CXO Councils include:
- **Chief Acquisition Officers (CAO) Council.** Chaired by the Administrator, Office of Federal Procurement Policy at OMB, the CAO Council promotes effective business practices that ensure the timely delivery of best value products and services to the agencies; achieve public policy objectives; and further integrity, fairness, competition, and openness in the federal acquisition system.
- **Chief Financial Officers (CFO) Council.** Chaired by the Controller of the Office of Federal Financial Management at OMB, the CFO Council advises and coordinates the member agencies' activities on such matters as consolidating and modernizing financial systems, improving financial information quality, financial data and information standards, internal controls, legislation affecting financial operations and organizations, and any other financial management matter.
- **Chief Human Capital Officers (CHCO) Council.** Chaired by the Director of the Office of Personnel Management (OPM), the CHCO Council advises and collaborates with OPM and other stakeholders to create human capital management strategies that attract, develop, and retain a high-performing, engaged, and diverse federal workforce.
- **Chief Information Officers (CIO) Council.** Chaired by the Federal Chief Information Officer at OMB, the CIO Council's mission is to improve practices related to the design, acquisition, development, modernization, use, sharing, and performance of federal government information resources.
- **Performance Improvement Council (PIC).** Chaired by the Associate Director for Performance and Personnel Management at OMB, the PIC serves agency Performance Improvement Officers by assisting with implementing the Government Performance and Results Modernization Act, facilitating the sharing of effective performance practices across government, deepening performance improvement capabilities within the federal workforce, and resolving cross-cutting performance issues.
- **President's Management Council (PMC).** Chaired by the Deputy Director for Management at OMB, the PMC advises the President and OMB on government reform initiatives, provides performance and management leadership throughout the executive branch, and oversees implementation of government-wide management policies and programs. The PMC is comprised of the Chief Operating Officers of major federal government

---

## Firsthand Experience from Dave Mader, Controller, Office of Management and Budget

I've served as Co-Chair of the CFO Council for the last several years and as Chair of the President's Management Council (PMC) during my tenure as acting Deputy Director for Management at OMB in 2015. This experience has reinforced my long-standing view that many of the "all of government" challenges such as cybersecurity, category management, and shared services can be effectively driven only through the collaborative mechanism of the CXO Councils and the PMC.

This horizontal integrating mechanism allows for several critical success factors in implementing new policy or program direction. First, the councils ensure that policymakers can gather input from key stakeholders in the functional community. Second, they drive consistent program or policy direction implementation across government. Last, the councils provide a forum for sharing best practices and feedback.

---

agencies, primarily Deputy Secretaries, Deputy Administrators, and agency heads from GSA and OPM.

## The Office of Executive Councils: A "Force Multiplier" for the Interagency Management Councils

In 2010, a dedicated team was established at the General Services Administration to increase the overall impact and effectiveness of the CXO Councils. The Office of Executive Councils serves in a government-wide capacity, providing management, analytical, and operational support to the councils. Their activities include:

- Facilitating annual CXO Council strategy sessions to set priorities that reflect consensus among agencies and OMB
- Managing CXO Council budgets to align spending with council priorities and maximize return on investments
- Conducting analyses to determine what's working (and what isn't) in CXO functions across government
- Documenting leading practices and sharing across the CXO community to improve performance, essentially building a "Center of Excellence" for federal management
- Training incoming CXOs at "boot camps" and providing development opportunities for "rising stars" in support functions

A final piece of advice for incoming agency officials: Even if you're not serving in a mission-support role, it's important to be familiar with the interagency management councils and to have a solid working relationship with your agency's CXOs. Too often, incoming leaders encounter what they perceive as obstacles when trying to hire and develop talent, acquire goods and services, formulate budgets, deploy technology solutions, or any number of enabling actions. It's simply not possible for agencies to deliver on their core missions if their support services are not working in concert with mission delivery. By gaining an understanding of your agency's support services and by involving CXOs in the development and implementation of agency mission strategies, your chances for success are greatly enhanced.

**Steve Brockelman** is Director, Office of Executive Councils, General Services Administration. **The Honorable Dave Mader** is Controller, Office of Management and Budget.

# CHAPTER FOURTEEN

# Office of Personnel Management

Linda M. Springer

# OFFICE OF PERSONNEL MANAGEMENT

*By Linda M. Springer*

The Office of Personnel Management's (OPM) purpose is almost unique in the federal government—it exists to serve other agencies. Its roots date back to the 1883 Civil Service Act, which established that merit-based hiring for federal employees be administered by a Civil Service Commission. The Civil Service Reform Act of 1978 distributed the commission's expanded responsibilities to three new agencies: the Merit Systems Protection Board, the Federal Labor Relations Authority, and OPM, which became responsible for the government workforce's personnel management. With a portfolio that ranges from personnel policy design and management, to benefit programs and performance management guidelines, to leadership development and human capital strategic planning services, OPM supports the people who execute your agency's mission.

While its name might imply otherwise, OPM supports the worldwide federal workforce's personnel management. It is led by a Director and Deputy Director who are political appointees, however career officials who have years of experience assisting agencies with human capital challenges carry out most of the agency's work. In addition to its responsibilities for policies, programs, guidelines, and workforce flexibilities that span administrations, OPM advises and leads presidential initiatives to address emerging workforce needs and performance issues.

## How OPM Interacts with Your Agency

OPM engages with agencies in multiple ways, driven in part by the nature of the service. Human capital strategy and workforce management issues have dedicated OPM personnel with specific experience with your agency, in addition to their professional expertise. Other OPM officials will handle issues, such as benefit administration, with multiple agency clients.

Your department or agency will likely have its own personnel function led by a Chief Human Capital Officer (CHCO). While some CHCOs are political appointees, many are career officials; if they are not, a career deputy CHCO typically will be in place to provide continuity and institutional knowledge from one administration to another. Through interacting with OPM, these leaders have a current understanding of personnel practices and tools to assist you and the agency in maintaining a high-performing workforce. CHCOs also meet as members of an interagency Chief Human Capital Officers Council, chaired by OPM, to engage in collaborative initiatives and insight sharing.

The President's Management Council (PMC) is another venue for interaction. The PMC consists of department Deputy Secretaries and other senior administration officials, including the Director of OPM, who engage with their counterparts on management issues, including those related to the workforce.

Because the overwhelming majority of the federal workforce is based outside the National Capital Region (Washington, D.C.), some of your agency's staff likely will be included in that group. OPM's field offices around the country provide local personnel management services. Federal Executive Boards supplement the work of those offices. The 28 boards across the country are comprised of local agency representatives and provide an opportunity for interagency dialogue and coordination on key issues such as continuity of operations.

In all these relationships, your, or more typically your human capital leaders', participation will enable you to be informed and to advocate directly with OPM on behalf of your agency.

## OPM Can Be a Resource for You

Your success as an agency leader is directly dependent upon having the personnel to perform successfully. Understanding human capital strengths and gaps is a critical dimension of your agency's strategic, operational, and budget planning. Building on strengths and addressing gaps will likely require using flexibilities and other capabilities to support workforce recruitment, retention, development, and reward.

OPM can assist you in this undertaking. It has proven diagnostic tools and planning methodologies that have been refined by years of working with departments and agencies like yours. These services incorporate leading human capital management practices with a particular understanding of the federal government environment's unique characteristics. Having an experienced resource to help you avoid missteps that can result from applying well-intentioned, but inappropriate, solutions to government workforce planning will prove invaluable in helping you lead your agency effectively. OPM is that resource.

## Partnering with OPM to Make Change

If you invite OPM to partner with you to design a workforce management plan that is informed by the full range of options available, you can optimize the outcome and timeliness of having a team capable of accomplishing your agency's mission.

This can be particularly valuable when unforeseen events emerge that expand the agency's responsibilities beyond what you had anticipated. These demands will often be time sensitive and require people with special skills and experience. Identifying such individuals, both within and external to your agency, in rapid fashion can be facilitated by engaging OPM to put its resources to work for you.

One of your first priorities should be to reach out to the OPM Director and Deputy Director. Whether the objectives you are responsible for achieving are routine or critical, you will only be successful if your agency's workforce is ready to execute. Having an established relationship with your counterpart at OPM will provide you a direct advisor who understands the administration's initiatives and can provide guidance for managing the most critical resource in your strategy—the people whom you lead.

---

**The Honorable Linda Springer** is a former Director of the Office of Personnel Management. She also served as Controller and head of the Office of Federal Financial Management in the Office of Management and Budget.

# CHAPTER FIFTEEN

# Citizens

Matt Leighninger

# CITIZENS

*By Matt Leighninger*

Changes in everyday people's attitudes and capacities have brought great opportunities, and great challenges, to the relationship between citizens and the federal government. The negatives, such as low approval ratings, contentious public meetings, and critical comments online, are currently more apparent than the positives. But better forms of public engagement offer new hope for improving the relationship and tapping the unprecedented civic capacity of 21st century citizens.

## Four Trends Affecting Citizen Engagement Today

**Citizens now have more opportunities and channels to engage.** We are experiencing historically low levels of trust in the federal government. People are more likely to protest against decisions or policies they don't like by using social media and other online venues as well as traditional engagement settings like public hearings and town hall meetings. But the flip side of this trend is that citizens are also making increasingly sophisticated contributions to the governance and improvement of their communities, sometimes with the use of online tools and other times through old-fashioned organizing and sweat equity.

**The shelf life of electoral mandates is shorter.** One common trap for winning candidates and new appointees is to think that elections empower them to enact a certain set of policies. But it is increasingly clear that electoral mandates are short-lived. About six months after an election, citizens usually begin to question the new administration's actions, and it becomes clear that there may not be sufficient political will to enact new policies. It has become very difficult, therefore, to transition from campaigning to governing. Most federal agencies and most members of Congress have weak and uncertain relationships with their constituents.

**Engagement practices have evolved into two main forms: "thick" and "thin."** "Thick" engagement is intensive, informed, and deliberative. It relies on small group settings, either online or offline, in which people share their experiences, consider a range of views or policy options, and decide how they want to help solve problems.

"Thin" engagement is faster, easier, and potentially viral. It encompasses a range of mainly online activities that allow people to express their opinions, make choices, or affiliate themselves with a particular group or cause. Examples of thin engagement have proliferated dramatically, while thick engagement has not grown as quickly.

Thick and thin forms have different strengths and limitations, and they complement each other well—the term "multichannel" is often used to describe participation that includes both kinds of opportunities. However, there are not many examples of federal agencies using multichannel engagement processes or approaches.

**The hope and high expectations of open government initiatives have not been realized.** Because of the language about citizenship and the engagement used by the Obama 2008 presidential campaign, there were high hopes that the Obama Administration would be a pioneer in using online tools for engagement. Those expectations were raised even further by the initial work on the national Open Government Plan. However, while agencies have shared more data and become somewhat more transparent, "Advances in the arena of public participation have been disappointing," writes Dr. Tina Nabatchi, an observer of Open Government Initiatives.

In fact, the United States now seems to have fallen behind countries like Brazil and India in the realm of democratic innovation. Brazilian citizens can now use online vehicles like e-democracia, as well as face-to-face engagement opportunities such as their federal policy conferences, to deliberate and make recommendations in a way that feeds into the policymaking process. In contrast, Americans are still limited mainly to thin forms of engagement, such as entering competitions or accessing information from federal agencies. This failure to provide richer opportunities for engagement has led to greater disillusionment among civic technology advocates and among citizens themselves.

## Recommendations for New Political Appointees

**Recommendation One: Think about engagement from the citizens' point of view.** Most government agencies that try to engage the public have specific goals in mind: the need to inform citizens, for example, or the need to gather input on a particular plan or policy decision. But citizens have their own goals, such as to:
- Share information among themselves
- Suggest new ways for sharing information
- Take action on the issue being addressed
- Participate in decision making

Citizens may also be compelled to participate for a more basic, social reason: An engagement opportunity allows them to meet people, interact with people they already know, and is generally enjoyable. Engagement doesn't usually work well unless it meets the goals of both the "engagers" and the potentially "engaged."

**Recommendation Two: In each engagement opportunity, include an invitation to another.** One aspect of moving to a more citizen-centered view of engagement is recognizing that people have diverse interests, and that participating in one venue may inspire them to engage in another. Abhi Nemani, a prominent civic technologist who was the first Chief Data Officer for the

City of Los Angeles, has called for more coherent thinking about systems of engagement, not just isolated meetings or online platforms. He offers the image of Lego blocks that can be assembled to create a stronger infrastructure for public participation. One aspect of this system would be that each civic opportunity a person engages in provides an invitation to another; for example, filling out a survey triggers an invite to an upcoming public meeting. Nemani calls this a "civic upsell" approach.

**Recommendation Three: Build on and help support engagement at the local level.** Agencies, public officials, and other leaders seldom collaborate when trying to engage the public; more often, each group of "engagers" works alone to involve citizens in a relatively narrow set of issues. Collaboration between federal agencies and local governments, school systems, and other organizations is even more rare. Local entities are generally better able to create sustained forums for engagement, both online and offline. By supporting the work of state and local government, federal agencies will have better conduits for reaching citizens.

**Recommendation Four: Raise the level of engagement skill in your agency.** Agency officials and employees who see the merits of engagement often lack the knowledge, skills, and abilities to launch effective and meaningful programs. To help build their capacity, agencies could take several steps, including:

- Identifying a participation "champion"
- Supporting opportunities for training and continuing education
- Creating and sharing engagement materials
- Creating platforms that collect and report engagement examples and innovations
- Supporting communities of practice

## How Will You Know That You Were Successful?

**Citizens are engaging.** Fortunately, there is some good news from recent research on engagement and citizenship. First, it is clearer than ever that people will engage if they think it will make a difference, either in their own lives or by having an impact on public decision making. Recruiting participants is usually the most difficult task in public engagement, because people are busy and because they are not optimistic that their participation will make a difference. There is now a wide range of research and practitioner experiences to suggest that federal agencies can overcome those doubts and bring large, diverse numbers of people to the table.

**Engagement is having well-documented impacts.** This is particularly true of thicker, more deliberative kinds of engagement, which are more time-consuming but also more meaningful and powerful. These impacts include:

- Citizen learning (as well as public official, staff, and other expert learning)
- Greater civility in public discussions

- Higher levels of trust, attachment, and collective efficacy
- Increased elected official accountability
- Greater citizen volunteerism to solve public problems
- New leader development
- Public policies that more accurately reflect what citizens want and enjoy broader public support

There is also evidence from other countries that sustained engagement has other long-term impacts, such as:
- Higher tax compliance
- Lower levels of corruption
- Lower levels of infant mortality and other health indicators
- Higher levels of economic development and lower economic inequality

**Deliberative engagement is having stronger ripple effects than you thought.** Even though engagement and its impacts have been more common at the local level, and practitioners have often despaired at the logistical and political challenges of "scaling up" engagement to the national level, there are some encouraging data to consider. First, participants in well-structured deliberative forums seem to carry their ideas and learning into much broader circles of friends, relatives, and colleagues. Second, voters seem to be swayed by the recommendations (published in voter guides) produced by a randomly selected set of their peers through a deliberative process. There is a stronger basis, therefore, for the notion that we can "aggregate" multiple engagements as part of a national process.

**Combining "thick" and "thin" forms of engagement is having an impact.** The experience of Creating Community Solutions (CCS), a component of the National Dialogue on Mental Health, demonstrates this point, even though the Obama Administration did not want federal policy questions to be included in the process. CCS has included small deliberative discussions, large deliberative forums, metro-wide action-planning processes, and SMS-enabled face-to-face discussions called "Text, Talk, Act" that have engaged over 40,000 people. It is an example of a multichannel, multilayered national engagement process, with impacts ranging from changes in individual behavior to regional action plans on mental health with extensive political support and millions of dollars in resources.

## Conclusion

Changes in what people expect from government, and what they can contribute to governance, have made engagement both more difficult and more beneficial. The bar is higher than before: Rather than simply informing citizens, engagement efforts must show people how their input will be used, and if possible, tap into citizens' capacity for public problem-solving. Agencies should develop long-term plans for engagement that align with their missions and empower the public to help achieve those priorities.

**Matt Leighninger** leads Public Agenda's work in public engagement and democratic governance, and directs the Yankelovich Center for Public Judgment. Previously, he was the Executive Director of the Deliberative Democracy Consortium (DDC).

# CHAPTER SIXTEEN

# Unions

Michael B. Filler

# UNIONS

*By Michael B. Filler*

Many public employees throughout the United States are represented by unions. At the federal government level, unions are legally recognized entities that have been elected as the "exclusive" representative of employees within a defined "bargaining unit" that is certified by the Federal Labor Relations Authority. As a result, federal sector unions have a statutory right to negotiate over personnel policies, practices, and conditions of employment, and to provide representation in connection with disciplinary matters and other workplace issues. Organized labor also seeks to influence Congress and the White House over pay and benefits, as neither is by law within the scope of bargaining at the agency level (except for certain agencies exempt from pay provisions under Title V of the U.S. Code).

## Where to Begin?

One of the essential briefings you should receive in preparation for your new position is an overview on the state of your agency's labor-management relationship. In addition, building a positive relationship with elected union officials and representatives responsible for employees within your agency or department should be high on your "to-do" list.

Within your first two weeks on the job, you should schedule meetings with the appropriate president of the international union with representational rights for your employees (usually headquartered in Washington, D.C.), as well as the top elected officer(s) of that union's local affiliate(s) or chapter(s). It is not uncommon to have many local affiliates/chapters around the country, so the frequency and manner of your interaction with them must be taken into consideration.

Don't be surprised if you find yourself dealing with several different international unions. Given the size of federal departments, this happens frequently. Many of those unions also hold membership in a larger labor federation (e.g., the AFL-CIO or Change to Win), while others choose to remain independent. Moreover, some unions represent solely public employees, but most also have members employed in the private sector.

While each union has a distinct constitution, governance structure, and manner of operating, from time-to-time they may coordinate activities as part of a labor coalition. This is especially the case when it comes to political and legislative issues, when interests align and there is a commitment to act together on a special project, a campaign, or on an ongoing basis.

## What Have I Inherited?

Understanding workforce issues and departmental climate indicators, like the results of the government-wide annual Federal Employee Viewpoint Surveys, will provide you a useful scorecard on where your agency stands. As previously mentioned, discussions with labor leaders within your agency will also shed much light on the relationship, including where progress has been made and where personal/institutional barriers to success exist.

Early on in your tenure, you should set the tone of the labor-management relationship. It will take time, honesty, and commitment. The personal investment you make, and how it is perceived by managers, employees, and union representatives alike, will establish a pathway marked by collaboration or varying degrees of ongoing conflict. More importantly, it will send a message of how you truly view the employees within your organization—i.e., as a valued workforce doing its best to meet the agency's mission or one comprised of overpaid, uncaring bureaucrats.

## What Is an Effective Way Forward?

President Obama issued Executive Order 13522 in 2009, which directed the head of each executive department or agency that is subject to the Federal Service Labor-Management Relations Act to establish labor-management forums to improve the delivery of government services. In seeking to "… establish a cooperative and productive form of labor-management relations throughout the executive branch…" the executive order also called for creating a National Council on Federal Labor-Management Relations. Among its responsibilities and functions, the Council was required to develop measurements and metrics for evaluating department and agency labor-management forums. Further, the Council was to recommend "…innovative ways to improve [the] delivery of services and products to the public while cutting costs and advancing employee interests."

You should review published information on the Council's website (www.lmrcouncil.gov) to gain a fuller understanding of Executive Order 13522, and general guidance developed by the Council, in an effort to improve the productivity and effectiveness of your agency/department.

**Pre-Decisional Involvement.** The Council is co-chaired by the Director of the Office of Personnel Management and the Deputy Director for Management of the Office of Management and Budget. In 2011, the co-chairs issued a joint memorandum to the heads of executive departments and agencies on the importance of pre-decisional involvement (PDI) with unions. As provided for in Executive Order 13522, agencies are required to allow for pre-decisional involvement with unions in all workplace matters to the fullest extent practicable. This includes sharing information with union representatives and resolving issues prior to making final decisions on, or implementing changes to, personnel policies, practices, or conditions of employment.

It is important to understand that PDI does not replace an agency's bargaining obligation with the union; rather, it is predicated on the concept that ongoing interaction with the union can help to operationalize the labor-management partnership as envisioned by Executive Order 13522 and, thereby, result in more informed (and presumably better) management decisions by allowing for and considering employees' input via their union. One example explained in the next section is the annual budget process, where unions should be solicited for input.

**Handling Confidential Information Under PDI.** Budget-related discussions can involve disclosing confidential or sensitive information. The Council has issued guidance on how to satisfy the executive order without acting in a manner inconsistent with OMB Circular A-11 (which, in part, prohibits sharing certain information during an agency's budget development phase). One option is to seek your labor representatives' concurrence to sign written confidentiality agreements to facilitate budget discussions involving information that normally would not be made available. It should be noted, however, that unions can provide input on:

- High-level goals and strategies when the budget is being developed
- Implementation plans while Congress is considering the budget
- The use of funds once the department/agency's appropriation becomes law

**Employee Engagement.** In early 2014, the Council and the Chief Human Capital Officers Council (CHCO) collaborated to address the topic of employee engagement. The focus was to identify promising practices, barriers to success, and ways to measure and reward progress. By definition, employee engagement consists of emotional, cognitive, and behavioral components, which are distinct from job satisfaction. Greater employee engagement improves employee productivity and customer service, while reducing turnover and workplace accidents.

You must set the right tone and communicate clear organizational values and expectations with respect to employee engagement. A close review of data from the annual Employees Viewpoint Survey will provide useful information on a number of key indicators that reflects the degree to which your department/agency has a fully engaged workplace. Developing a plan of action is essential to achieving progress in this area.

**Metrics.** Executive Order 13522 makes specific reference to using measures to track progress. The metrics should be practical and easily understood in order to turn data into action. In its guidance, the Council identified three areas where labor-management forums can use metrics for ongoing evaluation:

- An agency's ability to accomplish its mission and deliver high quality products, services, and protection to the public

- The quality of employee work life
- The labor-management relations climate

You must ensure that your labor-management forum has periodic substantive discussions about these areas and submits a timely annual report to the Council, which is the result of a PDI-based consensus between the parties.

**Employee Performance Management.** The Council worked with the CHCO Council to issue a report entitled "Getting in GEAR for Employee Performance Management" to address human performance problems found in many agencies. The acronym "GEAR" stands for Goals-Engagement-Accountability-Results, and serves as a roadmap "...to create high-performing organizations [within the federal government] that are aligned, accountable, and focused on results...." The Goals of GEAR, as contained in the report, include:

- Articulating a high performance culture within each agency
- Aligning individual employee performance with organizational performance management
- Implementing accountability at all levels from the White House to the front lines within each agency
- Creating a sustainable culture of engagement between employees and their supervisors
- Improving supervisor assessment, selection, development, and training

You and your management team should use these as interrelated processes that, over time, will improve employee and organizational performance.

## What Will Be My Approach?

You should engage labor within your department/agency in a positive, collaborative way and treat the union's representatives as informed partners. If, instead, you or your management team consider the union to be an outside constituency, you may create a combative labor-management relationship with varying degrees of conflict, a divided workforce, and an ongoing need for third-party dispute resolution. You choose the approach that will produce the most favorable results.

*Michael B. Filler* *was appointed by President Obama in 2010 to serve on the National Council on Federal Labor-Management Relations. He has over 35 years of employment and labor relations experience at the federal, state, and local levels of government.*

# CHAPTER SEVENTEEN

# State, Local, and Tribal Governments

David P. Agnew

# STATE, LOCAL, AND TRIBAL GOVERNMENTS

*By David P. Agnew*

## Introduction

The intergovernmental system in the United States is complex and ever evolving: The structures themselves are varied across the country, and the relative power and responsibilities of different government entities are constantly shifting in response to new laws and political conditions.

As a consequence, there will always be significant flux in the intergovernmental system. At the same time, the overall effectiveness of government at every level is fully dependent on the different pieces working coherently together. Each cabinet department and independent agency at the federal level must work closely together in coordinating their intergovernmental activities.

The White House Office of Intergovernmental Affairs (IGA) is a key actor in the federal government. This office is uniquely situated to help make the overall intergovernmental system work more effectively. It also occupies a unique platform from which to lead the discussion about the critical importance of intergovernmental relationships, how to reduce tensions, and how to promote collaboration between the various levels of government. Working with elected officials, intergovernmental associations, federal departments and agencies, and other stakeholders, IGA is poised to lead this conversation in a productive direction.

Nearly all federal departments and independent agencies have their own intergovernmental offices. While this chapter will focus on the White House Office of Intergovernmental Affairs, many of the functions of that office will also be performed at the departmental and agency level. As a political appointee, it is highly likely that you will engage with state, local, and tribal officials at many points during your tenure.

## About the White House Office of Intergovernmental Affairs

As discussed above, IGA is an important tool for any White House seeking to advance effective governance and make progress for the American people. The office was established during the Eisenhower Administration to serve as the point of contact for state and local governments within the White House, an action inspired by the need for better federal, state, and local coordination during the construction of the Interstate Highway System. Over the years, IGA's role has evolved considerably. Today it plays an important role, usually behind the scenes, by helping to foster a productive and nuanced working relationship between federal, state, local, and tribal governments, as well was with other federal organizations.

Though IGA is relatively small, it serves an enormous set of constituencies, literally covering tens of thousands of elected officials across the country. During the Obama Administration, the office consisted of three core teams:

- **State government team.** This team is responsible for coordinating with governors, state legislators, and other statewide elected officials such as lieutenant governors, attorneys general, and state treasurers. In practice, much of this team's focus revolves around the creation of strong working relationships with governors and their staffs, as the federal-state relationship serves as the backbone for implementing many federal priorities and policies. The office also works with state legislators, particularly on matters of state policy.
- **Local government team.** This team is responsible for coordinating with mayors, county officials, and other local officials, and it maintains a wide and intensely local set of connections in America's cities, towns, and counties. On many occasions, the most important and direct impact the White House can have is through relationships it has with local governments, particularly in times of crisis. As President Obama said to a large group of mayors in 2010, "You're the first interaction citizens have with their government when they step outside every morning. The things that make our cities work and our people go—transit and public safety, safe housing, sanitation, parks and recreation—all these tasks fall to you."
- **Tribal government team.** This team is responsible for coordinating with the 566 federally recognized tribes. It works very closely with the Department of the Interior and other federal agencies to make sure that our nation's tribal government-to-government relationships are handled effectively and to ensure that tribal interests are well represented in federal policy debates and program implementation. This team also coordinates the Tribal Nations Conference, an important annual gathering of America's tribal leaders initiated by President Obama in 2009.

## Key Roles Played by Intergovernmental Offices

During the Obama Administration, as in many previous administrations, the White House Office of Intergovernmental Affairs served as an instrument to help government work better, and it worked closely with federal entities to achieve this objective. IGA, department, and agency intergovernmental offices play the roles discussed below:

**Personal relationships with elected officials.** Success for the White House IGA, department, and agency intergovernmental offices lies in creating and maintaining strong personal relationships with state, local, and tribal government leaders and their staffs. Without an extremely wide range of direct relationships, intergovernmental offices simply cannot do their jobs effectively. From the beginning of the new administration, intergovernmental staff will reach out to elected officials directly. Nearly every state, local, and tribal official will welcome these contacts, who will form the basis for cooperation and collaboration during the remainder of the administration. While much of this outreach will occur based on specific issues, it's important to realize that nearly every entity within the federal government needs to maintain relationships with, and an understanding of, the interests and needs of its intergovernmental partners at the state, local, and tribal levels.

**Basic communication and execution.** The White House IGA will typically spend a great deal of time and energy executing a set of core responsibilities that promote the efficient and effective operation of the government. Often, this involves communicating critical information in a timely manner, either from the White House to elected officials or from these officials to the President and other federal officials. During times of disaster or tragedy, this is of paramount importance. This is also necessary when the President, Vice President, or First Lady travels and needs to interact with elected officials. This daily flow of information and feedback—on programs and policies and situational details—is crucial.

**Moments of crisis.** Intergovernmental offices have no task of greater importance than coordinating aggressive federal assistance during a moment of crisis or tragedy. During the course of any administration, there will certainly be many natural disasters to deal with—including hurricanes, tornadoes, floods, and fires—as well as all too frequent manmade tragedies. The White House IGA plays a formal role in the decision to declare federal disasters under the Stafford Act, and it coordinates direct communication between the President and other federal leaders with governors and mayors in the crucial hours after a tragedy or disaster strikes.

In the days leading up to Superstorm Sandy, IGA helped coordinate direct contact with governors, mayors, and tribal leaders to prepare for the storm's arrival. In the storm's aftermath, IGA helped coordinate a massive federal response carried out by an unprecedented government-wide push for assistance. These efforts were designed to supplement and enhance the strong federal structures that existed at the Federal Emergency Management Agency (FEMA) and other federal agencies.

**Partnerships with the intergovernmental associations**. IGA also serves as the lead federal engagement coordinator with a wide range of organizations that play a pivotal role in promoting effective governance. These organizations include:

- National Governors Association (NGA)
- U.S. Conference of Mayors (USCM)
- National League of Cities (NLC)
- National Association of Counties (NACo)
- National Conference of State Legislatures (NCSL)
- Council of State Governments (CSG)
- National Conference of American Indians (NCAI)

These organizations convene their members to learn from each other, seek changes to federal policy, and educate Congress and the administration on their constituents' key issues. Each organization has a series of large meetings: typically a winter meeting in Washington, D.C., and a summer meeting in another city. These gatherings are important moments for intergovernmental offices to cultivate relationships, solicit direct feedback, and showcase administration priorities and leaders.

**A bipartisan voice**. At a time of increased polarization in Congress, IGA has a unique and valuable opportunity to work across party lines. During the Obama Administration, IGA worked to create positive relationships with Republican governors and mayors. Officials at these levels of government are accustomed to collaborating across party lines, and they always appreciate federal officials willing to work with them to get something done. This bipartisan collaboration is also very important at the local level, and state and local officials are usually very willing to look beyond partisanship to achieve results for their citizens.

**Collaboration on policy development and implementation**. One of the most important and useful roles of intergovernmental offices is to advance overall cooperation between the different levels of government. State, local, and tribal officials are often frustrated by what they see as a lack of collaboration with federal agencies, and they frequently ask IGA staff for help. The IGA team can quite often play a key role in facilitating a solution by using knowledge of policy issues and relationships with appropriate federal officials. During the implementation of the Recovery Act, for example, one of IGA's responsibilities was to organize regular calls with Vice President Biden and groups of mayors, county officials, and governors.

**Special task forces and committees**. Creating special task forces and committees comprised of state, local, and tribal leaders provides the White House IGA a unique opportunity to solicit meaningful input and influence federal policy and action. In 2013, President Obama created the President's State, Local, and Tribal Leaders Task Force on Climate Preparedness and Resilience. Comprised of eight governors, 16 mayors, and two tribal officials, the task force members gathered input from their fellow elected officials and considered ways that the federal government could more effectively partner with them to prepare for and combat the impacts of climate change. This sort of formal, bipartisan collaboration can be an important tool to gather information widely and galvanize federal policy changes and action. Agency officials will be expected to play leading roles in these types of initiatives, and they will necessarily provide much of the staff support needed to make these initiatives successful.

## Recommendation

The White House Office of Intergovernmental Affairs, department, and agency intergovernmental offices must create mechanisms for aggressive two-way communication. Given the breadth of the state, local, and tribal constituencies, it's important for all federal government offices involved in intergovernmental activities to create strong, flexible, and robust systems for communication between every level of government.

These communication systems must allow information to flow to the White House, as well as departments and agencies, from elected officials across the country, and conversely to allow the federal government to communicate information directly to these elected officials. Nearly every form of communication—including social media, conference calls, video calls, emails, and face-to-face meetings—will play crucial roles in the daily flow of back and forth information.

**David P. Agnew** *is Managing Director for Government Affairs at Macquarie Infrastructure & Real Assets (MIRA) in New York. Previously, he served as White House Director of Intergovernmental Affairs and Deputy Assistant to the President for President Barack Obama and as a top aide to Charleston, South Carolina, Mayor Joseph P. Riley, Jr.*

# CHAPTER EIGHTEEN

# Interest Groups and Associations

Stan Soloway

# INTEREST GROUPS AND ASSOCIATIONS

*By Stan Soloway*

As a political appointee, you will be faced with making scores of decisions, often on complex, highly charged issues. Needless to say, there are many individuals and groups (both inside and outside of government) who would like to influence your decisions. As such, a key challenge you will face is evaluating the quality of information that will underpin your decisions. After all, seeking, parsing, and synthesizing information into an actionable framework is an integral part of leadership. Think of it as data analytics. Collecting the data is the first, vital step. Then you, as a leader, need to decide what to do with it and what it all means.

It is also axiomatic that your time is precious and information overload is a constant risk. That's where interest groups and associations can be of real value. By definition, their role is to provide perspectives from across one stakeholder community—be it an industry (generally represented by a trade association) or a profession (generally represented by a professional association). As such, they can serve as important resources and can become one-stop shops that enable you to gain valuable insight from a wide range of interests without having to communicate directly with each and every member of that stakeholder community.

Of late, there has been far too much of the opposite behavior. Indeed, over the last decade or so the quality and scope of these communications has generally lessened, primarily for two reasons: fear of the ethics police and/or loathing the opposition. Neither are good excuses. Know the rules of engagement, but don't avoid them. Think what you will of your opposition, but recognize as well that they just might have some valuable input.

Make no mistake about it, as an agency leader you will rapidly be introduced to the alphabet soup of organizations representing your agency's stakeholder community, and all are not equal. Some are very good at providing value in the form of information and context; others are less so. You also set the tone. If your goal is for your agency to move out smartly with new ideas, then the worst thing you could do is to ignore or cut off input from the outside.

To optimize the value of outside interest groups, there are several good rules that you might follow—and insist that your key staff members follow as well.

## Rule One: Ask them before they ask you.

Every interest group has its own agenda. As long as you know what its agenda is, don't shy from engaging its members in the process of finding solutions to your toughest problems. Often, the best way to maximize the benefit of associations is to proactively present them with specific challenges or questions to which you are seeking answers.

The best organizations will respond with thoughtful inputs that reflect real effort on their part to both understand *your* priorities and needs and to provide substantive strategies for you to consider. Whether you agree with their solutions or not, this outreach allows you to quickly separate the doers from the talkers and to recognize those organizations where ongoing and open communications are of real value to you, rather than just a political necessity.

## Rule Two: Stakeholder consensus is not always the goal.

While it is helpful to have alignment with key stakeholder groups around important policies and other priorities, there are limits to the possible. Indeed, when it comes to driving change, some external stakeholders will be as resistant as your internal bureaucracy may be. Industries or professions are rarely monolithic, and some have even evolved in ways that mirror your internal bureaucracy.

In addition, different associations representing the same or similar industries sometimes have different points of view. Even within individual associations there may be divisions of opinion. Recognize this reality; don't be afraid to challenge it and, most importantly, don't shy away from asking for those conflicting perspectives.

## Rule Three: Make external communications the routine, not the exception.

Never before has broadening the communications aperture been more vital. As noted earlier, that aperture has become dangerously narrowed and the result is more conflict than collaboration—more digging in of the heels than moving toward solutions. Just about every government official and every interest group leader will tell you that the scope and quality of communications is at low ebb.

You can change that within your agency. Know the rules governing communications—when they have to be public, when they are subject to the Federal Advisory Committees Act, when there is an active procurement underway, and so on. But don't let anyone convince you that external communications are either prohibited or somehow unethical. Moreover, set the tone; open the aperture and insist that doing so becomes the rule in your agency.

Outside of government, collaboration and communication is the rule in the business world; the government should be no different.

## Rule Four: Be focused and structured in your communications.

Routine communications and dialogue are not the same as open-ended discussions. Informal, open-ended contact can have value; but when it comes to problem solving, the more focused and structured the communication, the more you will get out of it.

There was always an agenda when I conducted roundtable discussions at the Department of Defense. It was composed of specific questions submitted to me or that I had submitted in advance to the associations participating in the roundtable. These structured discussions were not staged or contrived but ensured we used the time and the opportunity wisely and effectively—and in a manner consistent with my department's needs.

## Rule Five: Be transparent.

Transparency and openness are essential. Communications in government do not exist in a vacuum. Even when you know a group is likely to oppose your policies or initiatives, engage them as early and openly as those who are likely to support you. Picking and choosing which organizations to engage is not an option. The more you openly invite varied perspectives, the more credible you will be as a leader. When it comes to contentious issues, this becomes even more important.

Listening to the "opposition" may give you valuable insights, blunt some criticism, or at least keep the lines of communication open. It can also help to eliminate those "surprises" that so bedevil political leaders. Don't be afraid to be open about your priorities and don't be afraid to openly discuss them with all interested parties.

## Conclusion

As an agency leader you are, by definition, a change leader. Your role is to successfully implement the President's vision and agenda. Generally, that vision and that agenda require meaningful change. These rules are common to any successful change management effort. They can help you achieve your goals, help inform your decision making, and enable the kinds of relationships that make our democracy work.

Managing time and information are but two of the most difficult challenges you will face. Interest groups and associations are key to solving those challenges. By effectively integrating them into your process, you can gain the benefit of diverse and numerous voices coming together. You will rarely be surprised and your level of knowledge will be enhanced.

---

*Stan Soloway is the President and CEO of Celero Strategies. From 2001-2015 he served as President and Chief Executive Officer of the Professional Services Council, the national trade association of the government technology and professional services industry. He previously served in the Clinton Administration as Deputy Under Secretary of Defense and Director of the Defense Reform Initiative.*

# CHAPTER NINETEEN

# U.S. Government Accountability Office

David M. Walker

# U.S. GOVERNMENT ACCOUNTABILITY OFFICE

*By David M. Walker*

There is one very important and nonpartisan federal agency with a major government-wide impact that will not be directly affected by the transition to a new presidential administration in 2017: the U.S. Government Account- ability Office (GAO). The head of the GAO is the Comptroller General of the United States.

You may have some initial apprehension regarding GAO. After all, GAO is the "Watchdog for Congress." As such, GAO has a critically important role in helping Congress oversee the executive branch. In addition to GAO's well- known oversight work, the agency is also in the insight and foresight business.

Specifically, GAO has insights on what federal government programs, policies, functions, and activities work and which ones don't. GAO is exposed to "best practices" and "lessons learned" across the federal government and from its counterpart audit organizations around the world. GAO also employs foresight by identifying key trends and challenges that affect the United States and its position in the world. These can help government address current and emerging challenges before they reach crisis proportions, while also capital- izing on related opportunities.

Furthermore, in an effort to lead by example, GAO engaged in a widely acclaimed transformation starting in the late 1990s. GAO's transformation offers valuable information and insights to other agency leaders who want to achieve major transformational change in their own agencies. Given these facts, GAO can be a valuable source of professional and objective information for new administration officials.

## GAO's Role

GAO is in the legislative branch. Its primary mission is to support Congress "in meeting its constitutional responsibilities to help improve the performance and ensure the accountability of the federal government for the benefit of the American people." GAO is comprised of about 3,000 profes- sionals with a broad range of credentials and experience. It is, in effect, a diversified professional services firm that is a wholly owned subsidiary of the federal government. GAO staff perform a broad range of services, including financial statement audits, performance audits, program evaluations, policy analyses, research studies, best practices guides, auditing standards, legal opinions, and bid protest decisions. Contrary to the perceptions of some, only about 15 percent of GAO's activities relate to traditional financial statement audits.

GAO seeks to fight fraud, waste, abuse, and mismanagement while also working to improve the economy, efficiency, and effectiveness of the federal government. GAO's activities span the vast reach and scope of federal government programs and activities. They can include a broad range of financial, operational, technological, and other matters that can affect such areas as financial integrity, cybersecurity, individual safety, personal privacy, public health, citizen confidence, and key sustainability issues (e.g., fiscal, social insurance programs, infrastructure, environment).

GAO has broad audit and investigatory authority throughout the federal government, including in connection with classified matters. Its scope, authorities, and rights have expanded over time. GAO's only significant scope limitation relates to reviewing how the Federal Reserve Board sets monetary policy.

## GAO's Major Products, Policies, and Protocols

GAO issues a range of products that can be helpful to executive branch officials during both their transition period and term in office. For example, each year GAO issues hundreds of reports spanning a broad range of subject matters. Some of these reports may relate to your new role and responsibilities. Typically, about two-thirds of GAO's reports contain recommendations and 80 percent of GAO's recommendations are implemented within a reasonable period of time. The financial and non-financial benefits resulting from adopting GAO recommendations are the primary outcome-based results that GAO uses to assess its own performance.

While the frequency varies, GAO can testify before Congress hundreds of times each year on its reports, as well as on other current and emerging issues of concern to Congress. Some of these testimonies may also relate to your new role and responsibilities. In order to promote transparency and accountability, all of GAO's non-classified reports and publications are publicly available and posted on its website.

Every two years at the beginning of each Congress (i.e., the beginning of odd numbered calendar years), GAO issues a High Risk Series Report that outlines a range of federal programs, functions, and activities that are at higher risk of fraud, waste, abuse, mismanagement, or otherwise not achieving their intended mission. The latest report was issued in 2015 and contained 32 items. Some of the items are department- or agency-specific and some are government-wide in nature. Importantly, GAO's High Risk List is a major input factor when each administration determines what its management agenda should be. In addition, items on GAO's High Risk List receive a high degree of attention from Congress and the press. As a result, new executive branch officials should pay special attention to any issues related to their roles and responsibilities that are on GAO's High Risk List.

In order to promote transparency, consistency, equity, and accountability, GAO also publishes written protocols regarding its dealings with Congress and executive branch agencies. These protocols outline the rights, responsibilities, and limitations relating to Congress, executive branch agencies, and the GAO. They can be found on GAO's website and should be studied to ensure that all parties meet their respective obligations, take advantage of their related rights, and hold each other accountable.

In more recent years, GAO has issued Presidential Transition Series Reports in various forms that address a range of management and other challenges facing the federal government. GAO plans to update the "key issues" section of its website for the 2016-17 presidential transition. In doing so, it plans to place greater emphasis on outstanding key recommendations. This information can be invaluable to new administration officials in transition planning and preparing for Senate confirmation hearings, as applicable. GAO's past and pending work can also be of great value to new administration officials during their tenure in office, especially in connection with recurring congressional appropriations, authorizations, and oversight hearings.

## GAO Engagement Acceptance and Review Processes

GAO has an extensive engagement acceptance process that it uses to decide what work to perform. This process includes considering a variety of factors. Importantly, GAO is required to undertake engagements that are mandated by Congress via statute or are requested by a congressional committee with jurisdiction over the matter in question.

As a matter of policy, GAO honors appropriate requests from committee and subcommittee chairs, and it treats requests by ranking minority members with the same priority status as committee and subcommittee chairs. GAO will consider requests from other committee members and non-committee members, but they are much less likely to be accepted because there is a significant supply and demand imbalance for GAO to do work.

GAO can also consider requests from agency heads or other parties, although these are rare. In addition, the Comptroller General has the statutory authority to initiate any engagements that he/she deems appropriate. During the past 20 years, a vast majority of GAO's engagements have been mandated by statute or requested by Congress. The balance of GAO's engagements have been initiated based on the Comptroller General's statutory authority and are typically associated with key issues identified in GAO's strategic plan.

The Comptroller General has the authority to issue "demand letters" and to file suit in federal court to obtain access to needed information, if necessary. Fortunately, demand letters are rare and GAO has only filed a records access suit once in its history. It is in the interest of the department/agency, GAO, Congress, and the American people to avoid such conflicts if at all possible.

## Dealing with GAO

Every major department and agency should have a GAO Liaison who is aware of all GAO-related engagement activities within his/her respective federal entity. When GAO starts a new engagement, its assigned personnel will request a meeting with appropriate department or agency officials to discuss the nature, scope, and proposed methodology for the engagement. This activity is intended to minimize any "expectation gaps" and help to facilitate a "constructive engagement" approach between all department/agency and GAO officials.

During the conduct of GAO engagements, GAO personnel will periodically brief appropriate department/agency personnel on the status of the review, including any outstanding records or interview requests, preliminary findings, and possible recommendations. Take care to avoid unreasonable delays in GAO obtaining access to needed records or personnel. Unreasonable delays can result in congressional intervention, demand letters, adverse attention from the press, and even litigation. At the same time, department/agency personnel should advise GAO of any actions taken in response to GAO's preliminary findings and possible recommendations. These can result in modifications to the title of or the content within a GAO report in a manner that is more favorable to the department/agency.

At the completion of a GAO engagement, GAO personnel will conduct an exit conference with applicable department/agency personnel. These conferences provide applicable agency personnel an opportunity to influence the draft GAO report before it has been issued. Once GAO issues a draft report, the department/agency will have a reasonable opportunity to comment on it. Any written department/agency comments will be included in the final report. However, GAO has the sole and independent right to decide what, if any, modifications to make to the report based on any department/agency comments.


## Recommendations

**Recommendation One:** Review and consider the transition information under the "key issues" section of GAO's website that relates to your role and responsibilities, as applicable.

**Recommendation Two:** Review other recent GAO publications that relate to your role and responsibilities (e.g., GAO Strategic Plan, High Risk List, major reports, and congressional testimonies).

**Recommendation Three:** Determine who your GAO Liaison is and the current state of your department/agency relationship with GAO, the status of pending engagements and related requests, as well as the status of any major outstanding GAO recommendations relating to your role and responsibilities.

**Recommendation Four:** Consider whether GAO's own transformation experience may provide valuable information to help guide any of your own planned initiatives.

**Recommendation Five:** Develop and maintain a constructive working relationship with GAO. Draw upon its extensive knowledge and recognize that GAO can be helpful in building internal and external support for needed reforms.

*The Honorable David M. Walker is Senior Strategic Advisor for PwC and former Comptroller General of the United States.*

# CHAPTER TWENTY

# Inspectors General

Earl Devaney

# INSPECTORS GENERAL

*By Earl Devaney*

New administration appointees are usually surprised to learn that their department/agency Inspector General (IG) was not selected by the incoming President. It is much more likely that the incumbent IG has served under a number of previous administrations. While it is true that most IGs are appointed by the President and confirmed by the Senate, only President Reagan attempted to remove all the IGs at the outset of his administration. The resulting firestorm of negative publicity has since served to make new presidents extremely reluctant to expend the political capital necessary to replace the independent "watchdogs" who, by law, report to both the administration and Congress.

But, before you can understand how to work with IGs, you first need to understand their role. Unfortunately, this is easier said than done. There is an old adage in Washington that, "If you've seen one IG, you've seen one IG." In truth, while IGs are all selected without regard to political affiliation, they come from an extremely wide variety of professional experiences and backgrounds and they are all different. There is, however, one common denominator shared by each and every IG that is the key to understanding how to foster a good working relationship with them: Independence is a key element of all the laws creating the IG function.

The aforementioned dual reporting relationship makes the typical IG value his or her independence above all other personal attributes. Even the perceived lack of independence has been enough reason for the Senate to reject some IG nominees. Armed with this knowledge and coupled with the following four tips, you can achieve a very productive working relationship.

## Tip One: Your First Meeting is Key

This should be one of the first meetings any newly appointed official schedules and it is recommended that it be held in the IG's office. By going to the IG's office, a new appointee signals his or her sincere interest in establishing a respectful working relationship. The normal response to this gesture is often a more candid first conversation about what problems the IG knows you are inheriting from your predecessor. It is also a subtle way of acknowledging the IG's independence from the rest of the organization. While it is critical that this relationship gets off on a friendly basis, it is equally important to remember that most IGs are not looking to make new friends. The experienced IG strives to be independent, firm, and fair without regard to political influence. Most recognize that if you want to be popular, the IG job is not one to have.

## Tip Two: Set Expectations

An experienced IG should promise you no surprises. That does not mean you will always know who or what an IG is investigating, but it does mean you shouldn't have to read about it first in *The Washington Post*. In addition, IGs should promise to be very responsive to matters you bring to their attention and to provide you with their results as thoroughly and expeditiously as possible.

In return, you should tell the IG that you understand and value the IG's independence and you understand that sometimes delivering bad news is part of their difficult role. It is also important to tell the IG you have an open door policy and that you do not expect the IG to have to work through your subordinates.

## Tip Three: Be Aware of IG Resource Issues

An underfunded budget and a shortage of staff in the IG's office are never in the best interest of the agency. Regardless of how uncomfortable some of the IG's reports have been, it is in both parties' interest to ensure that the IG's work maintains its integrity and high quality, unimpeded by a lack of resources. It is clearly in the administration's best interest if the IG is able to embrace new technologies and keep pace with added program complexities. To that end, the administration should make every effort to support the IG's budget request to OMB and Congress.

## Tip Four: Understand How to Respond to IG Reports

Your agency usually gets to comment on a draft IG audit report but rarely, if ever, on an IG investigative report. Often the IG may be willing to make changes before issuing the final version of an audit report and will include the agency's comments in an appendix. The final audit report will also include the

---

## The Council of Inspectors General on Integrity and Efficiency

The Council is a statutorily created council comprised of the Inspectors General of all federal agencies. It is an independent entity that provides professional development for its members and it also coordinates government-wide initiatives such as oversight of the 2009 Recovery Act implementation, or joint investigations of other problems concerning waste and fraud that might reach beyond the boundaries of an individual agency or entity.

agency's formal agreement or disagreement with the IG's recommendations. It is important to remember that agreements to IG recommendations are carefully tracked. Failure to follow up on those recommendations can prove to be very embarrassing to agency officials later at congressional hearings.

Because investigative reports are normally criminal in nature, they are never shared before being issued. However, that does not mean that the IG can't give agency officials a heads-up that such a report is imminent.

## Conclusion

The working relationship with IGs is a major challenge for any new administration official and a delicate balancing act for the IG. Inherent in that relationship is a natural tension, but that doesn't mean the relationship needs to be adversarial. There undoubtedly will be disagreements but they don't need to be disagreeable. Developing a working relationship with IGs is hard work, but the return on investment is well worth the effort.

**The Honorable Earl Devaney** *served as Inspector General for the Department of the Interior and Chairman of the Recovery Accountability and Transparency Board.*

# CHAPTER TWENTY-ONE

# Media

Tom Shoop

# MEDIA

*By Tom Shoop*

Congratulations! You've answered the call to public service and have taken on a leadership role in the federal government. In so doing, you've accepted the challenge of working in one of the least trusted institutions in America, if polls are to be believed.

But here's the good news: Perhaps the only people held in lower esteem these days than government officials are members of the news media. So you've got that going for you.

Serving at or near the top of a federal agency entails dealing with reporters, whether you like it or not. There's a reason why the First Amendment guarantees freedom of the press: Journalists are there to ask questions of government officials on behalf of the people they serve, and to share the answers widely. At their best, they act as the eyes and ears of citizens and inform them about important issues by serving as a reality check on official pronouncements. At their worst, well…

As you take office, you will confront a rapidly evolving media landscape. Once, dealing with reporters was relatively simple: Only a handful of major newspapers cared deeply about government operations, along with a small number of TV network news operations. Many media organizations have now transformed themselves into agile, digital operations that place a premium on eye-catching "content." As a result, the media is more diffuse, more fast-paced, and more ideological. Upstart outlets regularly appear and disappear from the scene, and the President of the United States is as likely to grant an interview with *Vox* or *BuzzFeed* as *The Washington Post* or *Fox News*. On top of that, individual "reporters" unaffiliated with any media outlet can break huge news on social media.

At the same time, news organizations are under intense pressure to run lean operations. Reporters therefore are less likely to have the time to understand how government works than they used to be, and they are more likely to take a cynical view of federal operations.

In short, dealing with the media is a much trickier proposition than in the old days. It requires time, effort, and a tolerance for frustration. With that in mind, here are some pieces of advice for making the most of your relationship with news organizations.

**Don't try to ignore the media.** More than ever, government executives have their own outlets for telling stories, from official websites to multiple social channels. That makes it tempting to try to cut out the middleman completely. But that almost always backfires. Even small news organizations can command large audiences, and stories—especially those that put government in a bad light—can spread more quickly and widely than ever.

**Don't be your own worst enemy.** One of the biggest changes in media-government relations in the past decade is federal agencies' clampdown on communications. Many are reluctant to share any information about their operations—even good news. Something as simple as getting basic information about, or interviews with, federal employees who have won awards for excellent performance can be like pulling teeth. Putting up unnecessary barriers leads to decreased trust and increased cynicism. Especially in this day and age, federal officials should look to spread good news as widely as possible.

**Let your experts speak.** The best way to get your agency's message out is to let the people who really know their stuff talk about their work. Empower your employees: Give them basic training in dealing with the media, but allow them to speak. Communications should not be the sole province of the public affairs office.

**Resist the temptation to hide.** When bad news strikes, it's imperative to get your side of the story out quickly and thoroughly. If you don't, reporters will assume you have something to hide. If you simply can't comment on a story because of an agency policy, be direct about it. Don't string reporters along in the hopes they'll give up. They'll just find somebody else to talk about you.

**Set the ground rules clearly.** Unless a reporter has agreed in advance that what you say is off the record, you are on the record (as well you should be—you're a public official, after all). The definitions of terms like "on background" and "not for attribution" are squishy at best. So before an interview starts, make sure you clarify the terms of the discussion.

**If necessary, fight back.** By all means, use the communication channels at your disposal to point out when reporters get their facts wrong or simply reach what you believe are erroneous conclusions. Even better, do it with humor and grace. After House Speaker Paul Ryan was on the job for a couple of months, his staff published a funny blog post about the ridiculous number of "first tests" he faced according to news reports that relied on that journalistic cliché.

**Play favorites.** Journalists don't really like to talk about it, but they recognize that not all reporters are created equal. So while attempting to avoid legitimate inquiries is a bad strategy, it pays to work with those who approach their jobs with professionalism. If you find reporters and organizations that do a good, thorough, fair job, give them the access they deserve. You can choose who to trust.

Finally, remember that reporters are in the B.S. detection business. They only provide value to their readers and viewers when they separate spin from reality. So don't expect them to buy everything you're selling. But do make an effort to work with them. It will pay dividends.

*Tom Shoop is Executive Vice President and Editor in Chief at Government Executive Media Group, publishers of Government Executive, Nextgov, Defense One, and Route Fifty. He has spent more than 25 years covering government agencies and operations.*

# ADDITIONAL RESOURCES: THE MANAGEMENT ROADMAP

The IBM Center for the Business of Government joined with the nonprofit Partnership for Public Service to launch a Management Roadmap initiative as part of the Partnership's Center for Presidential Transition. The Roadmap provides management recommendations for new leaders aimed at enhancing the capacity of government to support key priorities and deliver positive outcomes for citizens.

The Management Roadmap is available at both the IBM Center website (www.businessofgovernment.org) and the Partnership website (www.ourpublicservice.org). The Roadmap includes recommendations and the following reports:

- *Managing the Government's Executive Talent* by Douglas A. Brook and Maureen Hartney. This report discusses the importance of leadership talent, presents key findings and insights on how political and career leaders can work effectively together, and provides a recommended framework through which the next administration can view executive talent.
- *Building an Enterprise Government* by Jane Fountain. This report discusses how agency leaders can coordinate and integrate activities to drive successful outcomes for the next Presidential term, and addresses models for enterprise government. The report identifies key challenges and presents recommendations for managing government as an enterprise that crosses agency boundaries.
- *Enhancing the Government's Decision Making* by G. Edward DeSeve. This report discusses how a new administration can quickly learn, adapt, and implement decision processes that help leaders make smart, timely, and actionable decisions. The report identifies tools and analytic capabilities available to decision makers and presents recommendations to help government enhance its capacity to make actionable decisions based on data.

- ***Encouraging and Sustaining Innovation in Government* by Beth Noveck and Stefaan G. Verhulst.** This report discusses ideas on how the next administration can drive, support, and sustain innovation as a catalyst for improving government operations and service delivery. The report presents a framework and recommendations on sustaining and scaling innovation in and cross agencies.

# ABOUT THE AUTHORS

**Mark A. Abramson** is the President of Leadership Inc. He was instrumental in establishing two cutting-edge organizations dedicated to improving management in government. In 1998, he helped create what became the IBM Center for The Business of Government and served as its executive director from 1998 to 2007. Earlier in his career, Mr. Abramson conceived and helped launch the Council for Excellence in Government and served as its first president from 1983 to 1994.

Mr. Abramson began his career as a public servant in the Office of the Assistant Secretary for Planning and Evaluation at the U.S. Department of Health and Human Services. In 1992, he was elected a fellow of the National Academy of Public Administration. Mr. Abramson is Past President of the National Capital Area Chapter of the American Society for Public Administration.

Mr. Abramson is the author or editor of 20 books and has published more than 100 articles on public management. He is co-author with Paul Lawrence of *Succeeding in Government: 50 Insights from Experience; What Government Does: How Political Executives Manage;* and *Paths to Making a Difference: Leading in Government* and co-editor of *The Operator's Manual for the New Administration* and *Learning the Ropes: Insights for Political Appointees.*

Mr. Abramson was a member of the editorial board of *Public Administration Review* as case study editor, has served as a contributing editor to *Government Executive,* and has served as a member of the Board of Editors and forum editor for *The Public Manager.* He received a Master of Arts in Political Science from the Maxwell School of Citizenship and Public Affairs at Syracuse University, a Master of Arts in History from New York University, and a Bachelor of Arts from Florida State University.

**Daniel J. Chenok** is Executive Director of the IBM Center for The Business of Government. He oversees all of the Center's activities in connecting research to practice to benefit government, and he has a special focus on technology, regulation, budget, and acquisition issues. Mr. Chenok previously led consulting services for Public Sector Technology Strategy, working with IBM government, healthcare, and education clients. He serves as Vice-Chair of the Industry Advisory Council Executive Committee, is a CIO SAGE with the Partnership for Public Service, and generally advises public sector leaders on technology policy. He most recently served as Chair of the U.S. Federal Information Security and Privacy Advisory Board.

Before joining IBM, Mr. Chenok was a Senior Vice President for Civilian Operations with Pragmatics and prior to that was a Vice President for Business Solutions and Offerings with SRA International.

As a career government executive, Mr. Chenok served as the Branch Chief for Information Policy and Technology with the Office of Management and Budget. He led a staff with oversight of federal information and IT policy, including electronic government, computer security, privacy, and IT budgeting. Chenok left the government in 2003.

In 2008, Mr. Chenok served on President Barack Obama's transition team as the government lead for the Technology, Innovation, and Government Reform group, and as a member of the OMB Agency Review Team.

Mr. Chenok has won numerous honors and awards, including a 2010 Federal 100 award for his work on the presidential transition, and the 2016 Federal 100 Eagle Award as Industry Executive of the Year.

**John M. Kamensky** is a Senior Fellow with the IBM Center for The Business of Government. During 24 years of public service, he had a significant role in helping pioneer the U.S. federal government's performance and results orientation. He is passionate about creating a government that is results-oriented, performance-based, customer-focused, and collaborative in nature.

He has edited or co-authored seven books and writes and speaks extensively on leadership, performance management, evidence-based decision making, and government reform.

Prior to 2001, Mr. Kamensky served for eight years as deputy director of Vice President Gore's National Partnership for Reinventing Government. Before that, he worked at the U.S. Government Accountability Office for 16 years where he played a key role in the development and passage of the Government Performance and Results Act of 1993.

He is a fellow of the National Academy of Public Administration and is a public member of the Administrative Conference of the United States. He serves on the budget and operations advisory committee of the National Science Foundation as well as on the editorial boards of the *Public Administration Review* and *The Public Manager*. He was the 2011 recipient of the Cornelius E. Tierney/Ernst & Young Research Award sponsored by the Association of Government Accountants.

He received a Masters in Public Affairs from the Lyndon B. Johnson School of Public Affairs at the University of Texas at Austin, and a Bachelor of Arts in Government at Angelo State University, in San Angelo, Texas.

# ABOUT THE IBM CENTER FOR
# THE BUSINESS OF GOVERNMENT

Founded in 1998, the IBM Center helps public sector executives improve the effectiveness of government with practical ideas and original thinking. The IBM Center sponsors independent research by top minds in the academic and non-profit communities. It focuses on the future of the operation and management of the public sector. Since its creation, the IBM Center has published more than 20 books and over 300 reports. All reports and other material are available free of charge at the IBM Center website: www.businessofgovernment.org.

The IBM Center has earned a reputation for a deep understanding of public management issues—rooted in both theory and practice—during its 18-year history of providing government leaders with instructive ideas that inform their actions.

The IBM Center competitively awards stipends to outstanding researchers across the United States and the world. Each award winner is expected to produce a research report on an important management topic.

In addition to the publications, the Center produces *The Business of Government Hour*—an interview program with government executives who are changing the way government does business. The Center also publishes *The Business of Government* magazine.

To find out more about the IBM Center and its research stipend program, to review a full list of its publications, or to download a Center report, visit the Center's website at: www.businessofgovernment.org.